Microprocessor Software Engineering

Concepts Series

OPERATING SYSTEMS

CONCEPTS AND

PRINCIPLES

John Zarrella

MICROCOMPUTER APPLICATIONS

© 1979 MICROCOMPUTER APPLICATIONS

All rights reserved. Printed in the United States of America. No part of this publication may be reproduced, stored in a retrieval system, or transmitted, in any form or by any means - electronic, mechanical, photocopying, recording or otherwise - without the prior written permission of the publisher.

2nd Printing, 1979

Published by MICROCOMPUTER APPLICATIONS

P.O. Box E
Suisun City, California 94585

ISBN 0-935230-00-9

PREFACE

In the many years that I have been associated with computer software and hardware, I have noticed that books have been written on two levels - one for the computer science graduate student and one for the programmer attempting to learn a language on a specific computer. Today, with the advent of microprocessors, a need has arisen for books which address a level intermediate to these existing works. This Microprocessor Software Engineering Concepts Series attempts to explore software engineering topics in a manner that is easily comprehensible to any reader who has a general knowledge of digital computers and programming.

It is virtually impossible to use or to design reliable software without understanding the concepts involved and without becoming familiar with the tradeoffs and limitations inherent in the design. This series is therefore dedicated to explaining some fundamental software engineering concepts, techniques, and terms, and giving you, the reader, a feeling for the scope of the design problem. With this background you should then be able to formulate your requirements in terms of software features, evaluate currently existing software, and determine whether suitable software should be designed or purchased. If you decide to design your own software modules, these books will give you a basic understanding of key software principles and will lead you to more detailed references in the field.

Of course, as in any technical field, terminology is a major stumbling block to the uninitiated who are trying to understand technical publications. Software, to a large extent seems worse than many other fields. In trying to reduce this confusion, each book of the series contains an extensive glossary of terms which deals with the software topics discussed in the text. In addition, terms defined in the glossary appear in **boldface** type when introduced in the text.

I would like to acknowledge the generous contributions of many of my associates: John Loram, Tony Stolz, Gary Lindstedt, Martin Newman, Jack Frost and Sam Schwartz who reviewed the manuscript and offered much constructive criticism, and Ramsey Zarrella who graciously typeset the final copy on her word processing system.

J.Z.

CONTENTS

1	Introduction	1
2	Operating System Overview	7
3	Tasks, Processes, and Contexts	19
4	System Services	29
5	System Support	37
6	Communication and Synchronization	51
7	Scheduling	59
8	Resource and Memory Management	65
9	Input and Output	77
10	File Systems	83
11	System Security	95

APPENDICES

A	Glossary of Operating System Terms	103
B	References	139
	Index	141

Chapter 1

Introduction

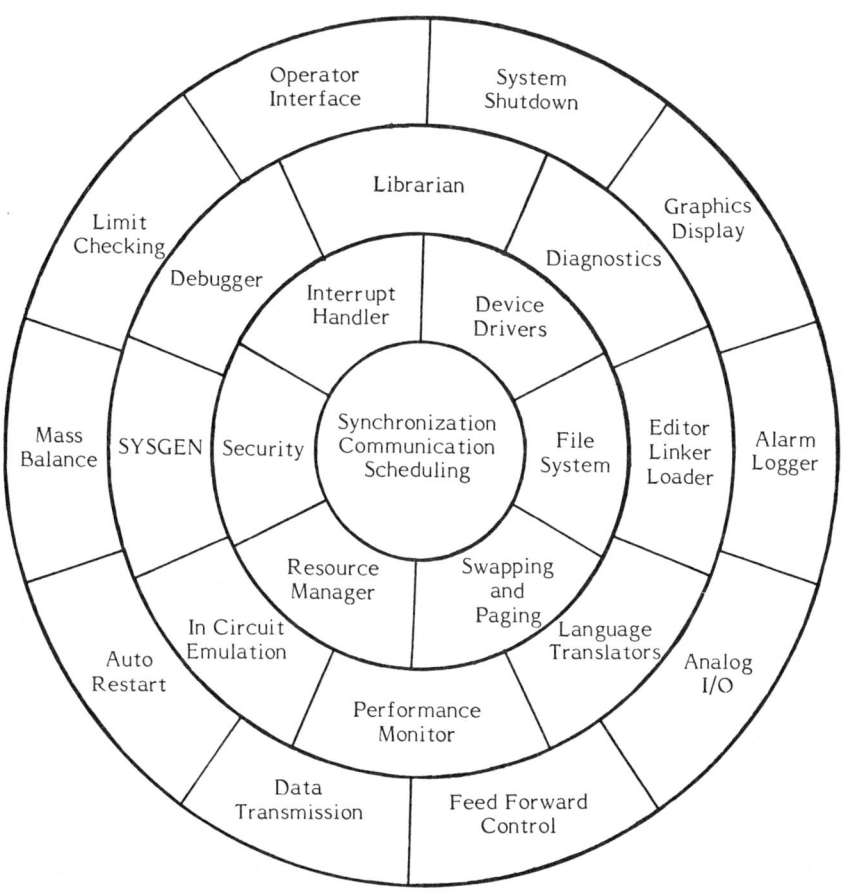

The best introduction to the concept of an operating system is a review of the historical basis of its invention. This will highlight the role of the operating system in alleviating many of the programming problems associated with modern digital computer systems.

Early Computer Systems

The early computer systems were operated by the same programmer who wrote the code for the software. At that time, each instruction had to be input to the machine via a set of switches. Needless to say this was a very slow and cumbersome operation and as more programmers attempted to use the system, two facts were realized:

1) Programmers had been spending too much valuable time performing the manual operations of entering their programs into the computer.

2) A productivity bottleneck had been formed at the computer since it required much more time to enter a program than it did to execute it.

At this point, higher speed peripherals such as card readers and teletypewriters were added to the system. But now, some **system software** had to be designed and coded to run these peripherals. The important point about this software was that it was designed, coded, and debugged once, and incorporated in a Read Only Memory (ROM) within the system so that each programmer could use this software. Whenever the computer was started, this software would allow the operator to type rudimentary commands such as *Load From Card Reader*, or *Start Execution*.

Operating Systems

This was the first example of an **operating system** or **executive**, a collection of system software which assists users by permitting a computer system to run more efficiently. In today's terms, the earliest operating systems were only utility programs to assist the operator (who was still the programmer) and not a complete system control program. However, once the concept was understood, progress was amazingly rapid. As computer systems became increasingly expensive and fast, efficiency and productivity became the watchword.

The next problem to be attacked was that of each programmer requiring exclusive control of the system in order to run and debug his program, a situation which led to scheduling difficulties and considerable wasted computer time. In order to lower the amount of unused computer time, each programmer was required to submit his program to a computer operator. In addition, the system utilities were enhanced so that the new "operating system" could load programs, execute them, and also peform special debugging functions. For example, if the program stopped running due to an error, the programmer could request a print out of the contents of system memory or, in some systems, a trace of instruction execution. The computer system could then run the next program while the programmer retired to his office to debug his program from the printout. Overall efficiency increased because the computer was seldom idle, even though the programmer's debugging task was harder since he was forced to recreate the program's execution environment from a single printout.

Since a special computer operator now actually ran the computer, a means also had to be invented by which each programmer could inform the operator of unique requirements (tapes or operator input) for his program. This was solved by adding control cards to his program which were interpreted by the operating system and displayed on the operator's console. A new dialect was devised for these cards, normally referred to by the IBM term, **JCL** (**Job Control Language**).

At this point complete, although still rudimentary, operating systems were available. Many computers in use today run with these systems, and many programmers still use them in the manner described.

Multiprogramming

Now that the programmer was physically out of the loop, many things could be done to the system to improve performance without altering the programmer's interface. One of the first things was to again improve performance by devising a way for the operating system to use any program idle time (e.g., while waiting for the printer) to read in the next program and store it on a disk drive. Prior to this, when one program finished executing, the operating system had to read the next program from the card reader. Since the reader was much slower than the computer, valuable time was wasted. By overlapping the card reader operation with the running of the previous program, the next program was ready on the disk by the time the previous program completed execution. This reduced the time required to load the next program from the disk to only milliseconds, whereas the card reader had taken minutes. This was the first use of a technique now known as **multiprogramming**.

It soon became obvious that this technique of overlapping execution of different programs could be generalized to work with any number of arbitrary programs and not just system software. Today most minicomputers and large scale computers utilize multiprogramming systems.

Microcomputer Systems

Microcomputer systems are now retracing most of the steps from computer systems of the past. Initially, the only available input was via toggle switches on the front panel of the instrument. Soon, small system programs called **monitors** were written to let a programmer interact with the microcomputer from a teletypewriter or CRT. Next, single-user flexible diskette operating systems were developed by many of the semiconductor suppliers and independent software houses. These were then used by manufacturers to build equipment with multiprogramming operating systems. Progress in this area has been swift since the field of Software Engineering had previously covered this ground before.

However, as fast as it has been, imagine the industry man-months that have been lost when hundreds of different companies independently developed I/O drivers for the same microprocessor and peripheral set. This, in a nutshell, is the rationale for operating system development - more efficient, profitable and reliable software.

Operating System Design

In the past, operating systems were designed as huge monolithic units, some over 128 thousand bytes in size. The design, implementation, and debugging problems associated with these systems were horrendous; small changes required multiple man years of effort, and fixing a single error often led to the generation of two or three more. Recently, however, the field of software engineering has improved tremendously on the methodology of operating system construction. Today, the most basic operating system functions of task synchronization, communication, scheduling, and memory management are carefully designed, implemented, and tested as a coherent unit known as the **nucleus** or **kernel** of the operating system. Functional layers of higher complexity software are then added on top of these basic functions, each layer utilizing only

Introduction 5

those functions (tested and debugged) residing in the lower layers.

With this construction method, custom operating systems can be easily implemented by modifying the appropriate layers of existing systems. Sophisticated operating systems have been generated in as little as nine man-months using this technology.

System Features

The final character of an operating system depends on the functions of the kernel and the capabilities of the subsequent layers. The following basic questions must be answered in order to either review an existing operating system or design a new one:

1) How do programs communicate with one another (Chapter 6)?

2) What rules are used to determine when to execute a program and which program to execute (Chapter 7)?

3) How should the system share assets such as printers, tape drives, and other devices among programs requesting their use (Chapter 8)?

4) What I/O devices should the system support and what level of support is required (Chapter 9)?

5) What data storage facilities should the system provide for programs and users (Chapter 10)?

6) What level of system security is required to prevent unauthorized access to programs and data (Chapter 11)?

Chapter 2

Operating System Overview

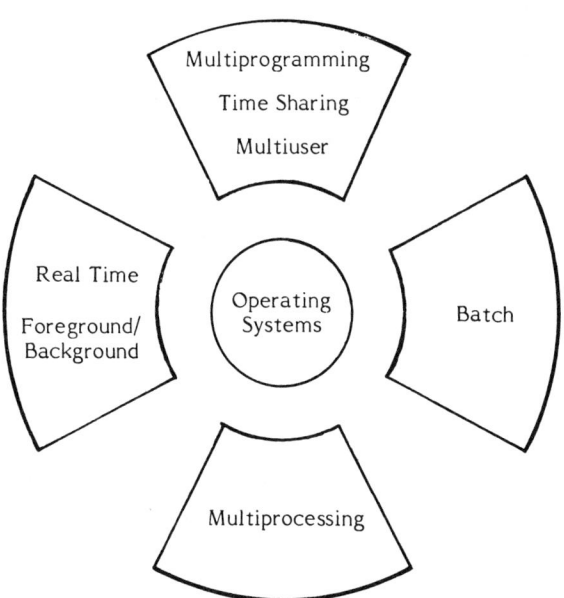

The operating system is the basic building block of digital computer software. Requirements imposed on operating systems differ from application to application. At the highest level, decisions made about the system environment determine the basic type of operating system configuration. Operating systems may be divided into four general classifications: Batch, Real Time, Multiprogramming and Multiprocessing.

Batch Operating System

Batch operating systems are the most straightforward in that they always execute a single program at a time, regardless of the size of the program or the time needed to execute it. These operating systems are usually found in the following environments:

1) University Computer Center - A small computer is often dedicated to student programs. Students learning the BASIC or FORTRAN languages load their card decks into the card reader and retrieve their listings from a nearby printer. Programs are usually limited by the system to less than two minutes of execution time. This eliminates the problems caused by incorrect programming (such as infinite loops) which could seriously slow the computer system. In practice, most student programs contain typing and other syntax errors so that they rarely require more than 5 or 10 seconds of computer time. In order to reduce idle time, some of these systems overlap card to disk transfers with program execution so that the next program is ready to execute by the time the previous program is complete.

2) Payroll Department - Within a small company, payroll functions are well suited to batch operation since a well defined set of operations must be carried out sequentially. First update payroll files for new hires, terminations, and changes in deductions. Then compute pay - regular plus overtime, and finally print checks.

3) Home Computer System - Home systems usually permit the user/programmer to perform only one function at a time. For instance, when the system is busy printing, the user cannot perform another function such as editing a file or running the BASIC interpreter.

Batch systems, while extremely easy to understand and implement, have some inherent drawbacks. Since each program is executed in order, once a large program begins executing, no other program, no matter how short, can execute until the first program is completed. To see how this affects operations, consider a very important program which takes two minutes to run. When submitted at 9:00 A.M., it is completed by 9:15. However, when submitted at 1:00 P.M. it is not completed until 4:00 P.M. because a four-hour job had been submitted just prior to 1:00.

With a batch system, the time interval between submitting a job and the time it is completed, known as **turn-around time**, is almost completely unpredictable. This leads to real difficulties for programmers trying to plan their work, and the computer center is almost always busy answering calls about turn-around time and job status.

Real Time Operating System

Some operating systems must cater to events as they happen in **real time**. These systems usually have very tight constraints on the time it takes the system to react

Operating System Overview

to a stimulus. In general, real time operating systems must *guarantee* this time requirement. Some examples of real time systems are given below:

1) Process Control - process control systems control the production of items as diverse as TNT, gasoline, breakfast cereal, and dog food. In all systems, a timely response to stimuli is essential. The time requirement can be as fast as a millisecond for dynamite and TNT processes to minutes for dog food production. Usually these systems periodically input various physical parameters (pressure, temperature, flow rate, etc.), apply digital integration and differentiation algorithms to them, and output control signals to valves and pumps.

2) Telecommunications - communications systems operate by transmitting a series of data packets along a single transmission medium. It is extremely important to guarantee that all characters of each data packet are received intact. If even a single character is missed due to a timing error, the whole packet must be declared invalid and retransmitted. This is tolerable only if it happens very infrequently. Thus, telecommunications systems must be designed to react within a very short time (less than a millisecond) after each character is received.

3) Military Command and Control Systems - the identification and tracking of friendly and hostile contacts, the interface to electronic counter measures, and the graphic information display to a pilot or commanding officer requires a computer system which can react quickly to new input and

update ranges and bearings as they change in real time.

4) Interactive Graphics - these systems interact with a user and must vary the display on a CRT screen in response to operator inputs. In many cases, as in aircraft design, the CRT view must be changed as it would appear to the pilot of the aircraft in actual flight. An architecture system, on the other hand, might require the viewpoint and perspective of a dwelling to change on the screen in such a way as to make it appear that the user was walking around the building or had just walked through a door.

5) Simulation - these systems require that all aspects of the simulation, which may include physical movement and acceleration of the user, occur in such a way as to be indistinguishable from the real experience. Simulation is used in flight training, transportation system design and process control operator training.

Usually real time systems have an execution time margin (of 20% or more) built in for emergencies, but during normal operation this is wasted time. Thus, real time operating systems often have requirements to perform very low-priority operations whenever the higher-priority real time programs are not executing.

Examples of these operations are:

    1) Statistical and Data Reduction Calculations
    2) Assemblies and Compilations
    3) Mass Balance Equation Processing
    4) Load Balancing Calculations

This type of operating system is often designated as **foreground/background**, where real time programs oper-

Operating System Overview

ate in the foreground with very high priority, while the background programs operate one at a time (in a batch like manner) only when the foreground is not executing. This type of construct enables the computer system to make excellent use of its computing power during normal operations, but to still retain enough spare capacity for emergencies or especially heavy periods of activity.

Multiprogramming Operating System

Just as real time operating systems utilize a foreground/background organization to make more efficient use of computer systems, a **multiprogramming** operating system permits multiple programs to share computer processing power. Essentially, this is done by permitting a single program to execute until it stops to wait for an I/O device, operator input, or some other event. When this occurs, the operating system saves all necessary information about the program in order to allow it to complete execution at some later time. The system then selects another program to execute and permits this new program to run until it stops. Thus, the system tries to keep some program running at all times so as to minimize the idle time of the system and to make overall operation more efficient. The rules by which the system determines which program to run next may be very complicated and are dealt with in Chapter 7.

Multiprogramming is a very powerful concept, since, when implemented correctly, multiple independent programs may be run together even though they have nothing in common with one another. This can solve the turn-around time problem previously encountered with batch systems since now a short and long program can share the system capacity. Neither may execute quite as fast as they would if the other program wasn't running, but their turn-around time will always be closely predictable because neither is forced to wait for the other to complete. Multiprogramming capability is also very useful when a computer system must perform many complex tasks simultaneously as is the case in process control applications.

A good analogy may be drawn between a multiprogramming system and a communication multiplexer. The communication multiplexer interleaves the *data* of many different *terminals* on the same *communication line* by making use of a standard *modulation technique*. In a like manner, the multiprogramming system interleaves the *execution* of many different *programs* on the same *processor* by making use of standard *scheduling rules*.

Multiuser Operating System

A **multiuser** operating system permits more than one user to operate the computer system in such a way that it appears to each user as if he has exclusive control of the machine. In reality, this is nothing more than a multiprogramming facility with sufficient security mechanisms to protect each user against another's errors. In addition, the system typically attempts to truly share the computer system power equally among the users. In many cases, this is done by letting each user nominally execute his program for a fixed period of time. These systems are known as **Time Sharing Systems (TSS)**.

The literature, especially that dealing with microprocessors, often refers to **multiterminal** operating systems. Though frequently confused with multiuser systems, they are significantly different. Multiuser operating systems always support multiple terminals, however multiterminal systems rarely support multiple independent users. Both multiterminal and multiuser systems are usually multiprogramming systems. An example of a multiterminal system that is not a multiuser system is an order entry system where, although hundreds of terminals are used simultaneously, each terminal is run by the same program, and each user is performing the same type of function. A user in this system would not have the capability of running a program other than *order entry* from his terminal.

Operating System Overview

Multiprocessing Operating System

Increasing computer power by adding more processing units enables a number of programs to actually execute simultaneously. A **multiprocessing** operating system increases system efficiency and throughput by coordinating the simultaneous execution of programs on multiple processors. In the general sense, these processing units may have distinctly different capabilities. In fact, machines have been built with separate logical and arithmetic processing units. However, most current multiprocessing systems utilize identical processing elements with identical memory access capabilities. There are two major reasons for this:

1) It is extremely difficult for the operating system to schedule program execution on processors whose capabilities are significantly different, especially where some of the processors cannot execute certain instructions.

2) Large scale integration has enhanced the capability of integrated circuit processing elements to the point where it is as inexpensive to have a general purpose element as it is to have a special purpose one. In addition, a general purpose processor can be utilized whenever a program is executed, while a special purpose processor may spend a large amount of idle time waiting to perform the particular types of functions of which it is capable.

One major exception to this rule is the **I/O processor** or **I/O channel**. An I/O processor is a special purpose processor with an instruction set that is dedicated to, and optimized for, input and output functions such as block data transfers, error detection, and interrupt service. The concept of these processors is very old as it was early recognized that I/O functions and general processing functions were significantly different. These functions could, in many cases, be performed simultaneously if processing units were available. A program typically uses an I/O processor as follows:

1) A special I/O instruction area is set aside in memory by the general purpose processor. This area contains I/O instructions that cause the I/O processor to perform the required I/O transfers.

2) The program executes a *Start I/O* instruction that commences I/O processor execution of the instructions in the I/O area.

3) The program continues to execute on the general purpose processor until it requires the I/O operation to be completed (the program is ready to operate on the data read from a disk file).

4) The program executes an *I/O Wait* instruction that causes the program to stop executing until the I/O operation is complete.

5) Normal instruction execution is resumed after I/O is completed.

To effectively use an I/O processor, a program must be structured in such a way that it starts I/O operations well before the data is needed and performs as much computation as it can before it uses the I/O data. This makes maximum use of the overlapping of general and I/O processor execution. This, however, is often an impossible task since I/O transfer times are not always predictable due to peripheral access time variations. Fortunately, the concept of multiprogramming again comes to the rescue. With a multiprogramming operating system, another program can execute while one is waiting for I/O operations to complete. Thus, both processors can be kept busy with very little idle time.

Operating System Overview

Load Sharing

When all processing elements within a multiprocessor system are identical, a program will yield the same results regardless of the processing element on which it is executed. This fact is used by multiprocessing operating systems to implement a philosophy known as **load sharing**. This technique attempts to share the computation load equally among all the processing elements within the computer system.

In a load sharing system, when a processing element becomes idle because the current program has completed execution or is waiting for I/O, the operating system selects another program that is ready to execute and starts it executing on the idle processor. Thus, a program may first execute on one processor, stop executing while it waits for input, and then resume execution on a completely different processor. Since all processors are identical, this makes no difference to the program, and permits maximum utilization of the computer processing capability.

Distributed Processing

The ease of design and small size of microprocessor systems has ushered in another era of multiprocessing system design. However, instead of identical processing elements, these new designs make use of the concept of **distributed processing** where each microprocessor element is designed for a specific purpose and accepts high level commands such as *integrate for five seconds* or *compute fast fourier transform* from other processing units. The design of these units is therefore concerned with optimizing the performance of their tasks, and a standard communication interface protocol (such as SDLC or a proprietary bus) is used to transmit commands and data between the processors and to coordinate their activities.

If each processing element of a distributed system is dedicated to a particular function and a central processor controls the operation of these elements, only one operating system is normally implemented (on the central processor). The other processors are used in a manner similar to I/O processors. On the other hand, some distributed systems contain more than one intelligent general purpose processor. In this case, each of these processors may execute under control of an operating system and assume control of the communication interface and other processing elements as required by the individual application.

Operating System Overview 17

Chapter 3

Tasks, Processes, and Contexts

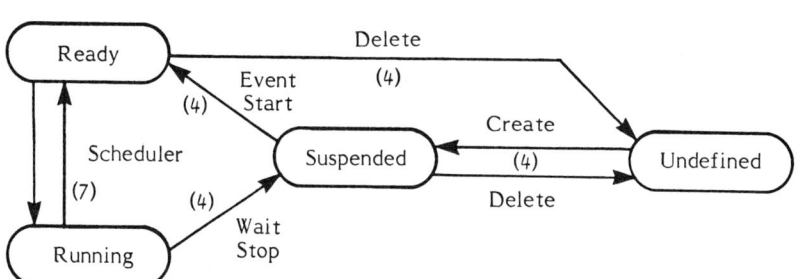

The most basic unit of software within an operating system is the **process** or **task**. A process or task can be loosely defined as a sequence of actions carried out one at a time. The following examples of tasks may help make this definition more clear:

1) A Time-of-Day task executes every second. It increments the current time and displays it in the corner of the operator console CRT. It has no input and generates a single output buffer each second that it sends to the console I/O task.

2) An Analog Input task executes when the Analog I/O subsystem hardware indicates a complete A/D conversion via an interrupt. This task performs the input operation and writes the data into a shared data area for later use by other tasks.

3) A Power Down task executes very rarely - only in the event of a power failure. This task is the highest priority task in the system. It runs without interruption and saves all volatile data on a non-volatile medium such as core memory, battery backed-up RAM, disk, or bubble memory.

Tasks usually do not perform all aspects of a function alone. In order to make the software more modular and easier to write, the function to be performed is often decomposed into many cooperating tasks. A good example of this decomposition is the Assembler function as depicted in Figure 3-1 which takes a text file from the disk as input and produces a listing on the printer, an error log on the CRT terminal, and an object module file on the disk.

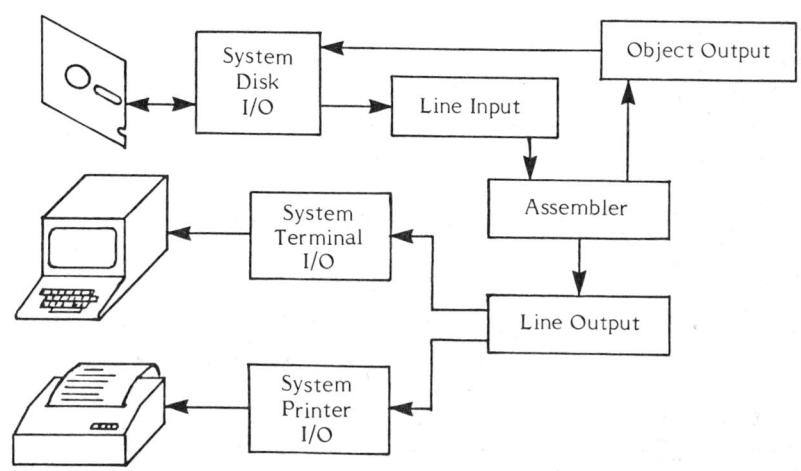

Figure 3-1   Decomposition of the Assembler Task into Seven Subtasks.

The Assembler function has been broken down into seven subtasks. Three of these subtasks, known as system services, are general in nature (dealing with I/O devices) and are usually supplied with the operating system.

1) System Disk I/O - a system service task which handles disk read/write functions.

2) Line Input - A task that inputs a text file from the disk and transfers this text, one line at a time, to the Assembler task.

3) Assembler - The main task that receives a line of text from the Line Input task, translates it into machine code, transfers the resulting code

Tasks, Processes, and Contexts 21

to the Object Output task, and passes the listing line and any error messages to the Line Output task.

4) Object Output - A task that outputs an object file to the disk through the System Disk I/O task.

5) Line Ouput - A task which receives a line of output from the Assembler task and prints the line on the printer. If the line is an error message, it also lists the line on the CRT.

6) System Printer I/O - A system service task that handles printer functions.

7) System Terminal I/O - A system service task that handles terminal read/write functions.

Within each one of these tasks, instructions are executed sequentially. When the Assembler task is ready for input, it requests a line of text from the Line Input task that reads this line from the disk. After performing its computations, the Assembler task passes an output line to the Line Output task. When this task has printed the line, the Assembler task transfers the assembled machine code to the Object Output task. A typical time line for these operations is shown in Figure 3-2.

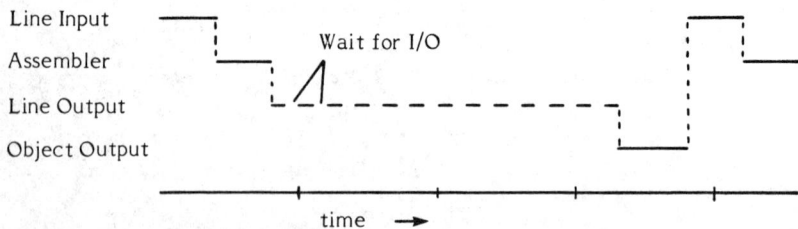

Figure 3-2   Assembler Task Time Line showing sequential execution of subtasks.

22   OPERATING SYSTEMS

The only problem with this execution scenario is that the Assembler task must wait until each I/O operation completes, while in fact the printer is so slow that while waiting for the printer to complete the line, the object code could be written to the disk and another text line could be read in preparation for the next assembly computation. To try to overlap these operations, most operating systems incorporate a multiprogramming capability where other tasks may be executed while a task is waiting for an event. This is where the concept of **concurrent** task execution comes into play. This essentially means that task execution may overlap in time. In a single processor system, task execution is interleaved since a processor can only execute one task at a time, while in a multiprocessor system, tasks may indeed be executing simultaneously. If the Assembler subtasks were written as concurrent processes, the scenario would change as described in the following paragraphs (see Figure 3-3).

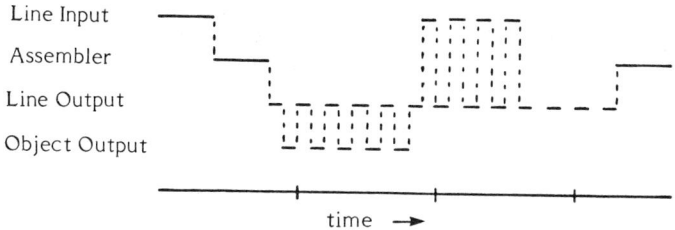

Figure 3-3   Assembler Task Time Line showing how subtasks may share processor time when written as concurrent processes; total execution time is reduced.

The Line Input task starts executing and reads a text line from the disk. It then sends the text line to the Assembler task. This action stops the Line Input task and starts the Assembler task that produces a machine code instruction. It then sends listing data to the Line Output task that starts printing. While printing, however, the Line Output task is idle for a large portion of the time required to print

Tasks, Processes, and Contexts   23

each character. During this time, the Assembler task again executes and sends the machine code to the Object Output task that stores the object code on the disk.

At this point, the printer finishes, and the Line Output task displays an error messsage at the terminal. Again, the task is idle for long periods and the Line Input task executes, readying the next text line from the disk file. As soon as the terminal finishes, the scenario is repeated. Executing in this manner substantially shortens total throughput time by overlapping task operations and by making use of idle time that would otherwise be wasted.

Contexts

When a task is ready to execute, it is placed under control of a system module called the **scheduler** (see Chapter 7). When the scheduler determines that a task should be executed, it starts task execution. If the task has just entered the system, the task is started at its **entry point**, a predefined point in the task instruction sequence where execution should begin. However, if the task had previously been running, the scheduler must restart it at precisely the point where it was stopped.

In order to restart a task, the operating system uses the task **context**. Each task has a context associated with it. The context of a task is the information that specifies the complete status of a task, e.g., registers, instruction pointer, and changeable memory locations. This context must be protected and/or saved when the task is interrupted for any reason so that it can resume executing at some later time without error. Often a small portion of the context is stored in system tables for scheduling efficiency. This block of information is commonly referred to as a **task descriptor** or **task control block**, and contains the task name, number, priority, state, and other status data.

Tasks are normally divided into three sections: code, data memory, and system resources. When a task is interrupted, it is only necessary to save the code section if it changes itself (e.g., rewrites actual instructions). This is called **self-modifying code**. **Reentrant code**, on the other hand, does not modify itself and does not need to be saved. Some systems in fact will reuse the reentrant code memory area of a task when it is not running and then reload it from secondary storage when it is restarted. Most data memory, on the other hand is changed by the task when it executes and must therefore be either saved or protected until the task is restarted. Real time operating systems often attempt to keep these data sections in memory. However, time sharing and other large systems where the tasks that are ready to execute are considerably larger than available memory, will perform **swapping** operations on these data sections. This means that in order to create more available memory for other tasks, low-priority tasks will be moved to secondary storage (disk, high-speed drum, or magnetic bubble memory). When these tasks are to be restarted, the swapped sections must be reloaded into system memory.

Some systems have a special flag associated with each data section that is set whenever any data within that section is changed. If the flag is not set when task execution is interrupted, the system can treat the data section like reentrant code and can free its memory area without moving the data to disk since it is the same as the data on disk from the last swap.

System resources must be treated in a slightly different manner than task code and data sections. If the task is using resources that must be used by the next executing task, all pertinent information about their use must be saved in order to be restarted without error. These resources usually include processor registers, processor status flags, interrupt masks, etc. However, this set of

Tasks, Processes, and Contexts 25

resources varies from machine to machine. For example, some machines have multiple register sets, and each task has its own set, so they never need to be saved.

Other system resources are simply left assigned to the task even when it is not executing because it would be very difficult or impossible to return them to their current state. Tape drives and printers usually fall into this category.

Task States

From the time a task is coded by the programmer and saved in memory or on secondary storage until the task is destroyed, it is in one of four **task states**. Tasks move among these states as they are created, begin execution, are interrupted, wait for events, and finally complete their functions. The following list details the four task states and Figure 3-4 depicts their interrelationships:

1) **Undefined** - Unknown to the operating system. A task is in this state before it has been created and after it has been deleted. At this point it is nothing more than a block of code in a disk file or stored in memory.

2) **Ready** - Prepared to execute on a processor.

3) **Running** - Executing on a processor.

4) **Suspended** - Waiting for an event. When a task is created or stopped for any reason, it enters this state.

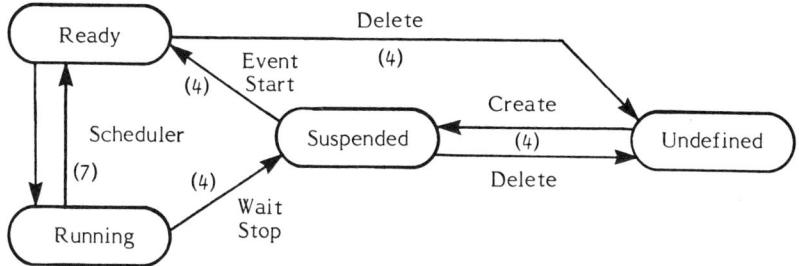

Figure 3-4 Task State Diagram illustrating the relationships among the four task states. Numbers in parentheses indicate the chapters where state transitions are discussed.

A task is not defined until it is entered into the operating system tables. Thus, a program coded and stored on a disk drive is in the **Undefined** task state until the programmer (or another task) informs the operating systems that the specified task should be entered into the system. Many systems which are dedicated to a single type of function have fixed tables of tasks, and these tables are often generated manually by the programmer. However, time sharing systems normally require the ability to dynamically enter and delete tasks from system tables.

Once information about a task has been entered into the system tables, the task enters the **Suspended** state, waiting to be started. When the task is started, it is moved to the **Ready** state which indicates that it is ready to execute on a processor. A system function, called the **Scheduler**, selects tasks from the Ready state and begins task execution whenever processors are available.

Tasks, Processes, and Contexts

As a task is executing (in the **Running** task state), several events can cause it to be stopped. For example a hardware interrupt could occur that required a higher priority task to be executed, or the task could voluntarily stop while waiting for a message from another task. When the task stops running because it is waiting for some event, it is said to be **suspended** or **blocked**. The task remains in the suspended state until the event occurs. Some systems permit a task to specify a maximum time limit so that if the event does not occur, the task will not hang indefinitely. When a task is forced to stop executing by an interrupt or higher priority task, it is usually placed back in the Ready state for later restarting by the scheduler.

Chapter 4

System Services

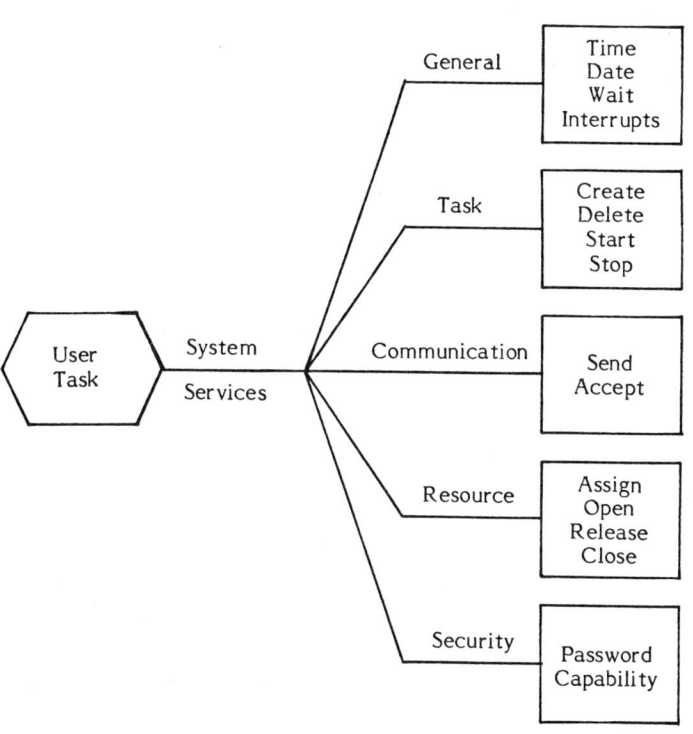

It is the responsibility of the operating system to see that each task is provided with the support it requires in order to perform its designated function. This support can be divided into the categories of **system services** and **system support**. System services are those functions that a task requests of the operating system while executing. System support includes programs and tasks that enable a user to design, implement, test, and execute tasks in an efficient manner. The topic of system support is discussed in Chapter 5.

System Services

System services provided by an operating system fall into five distinct classes:

1) General Services - Timing, interrupt handling, and data structure maintenance.

2) Task Services - Moving tasks within the system and providing execution facilities for them.

3) Communication - Facilitating data and command movement between cooperating tasks.

4) Resource Services - Granting resources to requesting tasks and driving peripheral devices such as printers, tape/disk drives, and terminals.

5) Security - Protecting data structures and tasks from damage and guaranteeing privacy to users.

General Services

All operating system functions are controlled by information stored in the various system-wide **data structures**. These structures may be **linked lists** of task information, **queues** of data to be passed among cooperating tasks, or tables containing access codes for file system structures. Special system software modules control all accesses to these structures in order to guarantee system integrity.

In addition to a variety of system tables, almost all operating systems have timekeeping capabilities. These usually take the form of:

1) **Time** - provides a task with the current time-of-day.

2) **Date** - provides a task with the date.

3) **Wait** - permits a task to be suspended for a specified time interval.

Finally, the operating system provides the most basic level of software at which hardware interrupts are handled. All operating systems provide the capability of triggering tasks based on interrupt events. Most operating systems also handle the saving and restoring of task contexts when an interrupt occurs, and many fit hardware interrupt priorities into a general preemptive scheduling scheme so that an interrupt event is treated in the same manner as other events. An example of this is an I/O driver task which transmits a character to a CRT terminal. It must then wait for the event: *completion of transmission.* In practice, this is usually a *transmitter buffer empty* interrupt from the serial communication interface (UART). The operating system fields this interrupt and sends a *transmission complete* message to the driver task.

Task Services

In order for a task to be properly executed, it must be known to the operating system. This is usually accomplished through a **Task List**, a system data structure that contains the names and locations of all tasks within the system. When a new task is created by a programmer or another task, a system service, **create**, is provided to

System Services 31

enter the task into the Task List. A complementary service, **delete,** is available to remove tasks from the Task List.

Without the ability to create and delete tasks, it would be impossible to add new tasks to the system without regenerating the system Task List. Usually systems operate so that on power-up they load the operating system and a set of user interface tasks into memory and begin execution. These tasks then use the create and delete services under operator command to bring other tasks such as assemblers or compilers into the system. Note that a task may be loaded into system memory without being added to the task list if the task is not intended to be executed. Many real time systems do not include create and delete services and require that all tasks be manually entered into the Task List when the operating system is generated. Many customers of these systems will attest to the difficulty and expense of adding new tasks in this manner!

Once a task is entered into the Task List, it is known to the operating system and can be operated on by other tasks. For instance, a system service, **start,** is usually available to place the task in the **Ready List,** a system data structure containing descriptions of tasks which are ready to be executed by a processor. Usually, operating systems are designed so that ordinary tasks as well as users at terminals may start other tasks. However, some real time systems only permit tasks to be started by the system operator at the console. The start service is usually very versatile and permits tasks to be placed in the Ready List either immediately, after a time delay, at a specified time-of-day, or at periodic intervals.

In a manner similar to starting a task, a system service called **stop** may be used to halt task execution and to remove a task from the Ready List.

The start and stop services are extremely useful in multi-programming and real time operating systems since control programs and/or system operators frequently start and stop subtasks based on external conditions. For instance, a foreground task may start a background data analysis task after all test data has been recorded. On the other hand, the system operator may start a system status task to execute every second in order to update the console CRT display with information about system efficiency, disk activity, and overhead analysis.

Actual task execution is controlled by the **Scheduler**, a system software module that determines which task in the Ready List should be executed next and how long it should execute.

Communication Services

In an operating system environment, tasks must frequently cooperate with one another since many functions are too large or complex to be performed by a single task. This inevitably involves transmitting commands and data from one task to another or sharing data between the tasks. All operating systems support some form of task communication although their techniques vary greatly. Most systems support two mechanisms, the first of which is a common or shared data area. Task access to this area is controlled by the operating system via synchronization operations as described in Chapter 6. This mechanism assures that tasks can't destroy shared data integrity by simultaneously updating the same data record or reading a record before another task has finished updating it. The second mechanism provides a facility by which one task may send data to another task, and permits the receiving task to suspend itself until the data arrives. This mechanism provides the means for a task to release a processor for use by another task until there is more work to be done. This capability is the basis for multiprogramming operating systems.

Communication services are discussed in Chapter 6.

System Services 33

Resource Services

Every computer system has associated with it a limited number of expensive assets commonly known as **resources**. Some resources may be used simultaneously by more than one task in certain cases, and others must be exclusively granted to a single task. Real time transaction oriented systems (order entry or accounting) utilize resource (file) sharing capabilities extensively while updating booking, billing, and accounts receivable information. Operating systems generally provide an **assign** service that tasks use to gain exclusive control of a resource such as a printer, tape drive, or terminal. Additionally, an **open** function is provided for use with disk files and other resources which must be shared. The requesting task is usually required to provide information on how it wishes to use the resource and the system then decides whether the task may share the resource. An example of resource sharing is the use of a disk data file. Multiple tasks may open the file for data reads. However, if the file had been opened for updating (data writes), no task would be permitted to open it for reading until the update was complete.

Complementary services of **release** and **close** are provided to inform the operating system that the task has concluded its use of the resource.

System memory is a special case of a resource to which a task is granted exclusive control since it is almost always severely limited in size and extremely expensive (even at current memory prices). Thus, significantly more complex allocation algorithms (discussed in Chapter 8) are employed to conserve this resource.

In addition to the above services, a good operating system usually provides an extensive file system (see Chapter 10) and considerable input/output support in the form of **device drivers** for common peripherals. These drivers are small software modules that handle hardware related I/O functions, interrupts and error conditions for the requesting task.

Security

Outside of military applications and special purpose systems, operating system security provisions have largely been ignored. Systems may be designed with either a **hostile** or **friendly environment** in mind. A friendly environment assumes that hardware and software have been completely checked out by the time the system is shipped or installed. Diagnostic programs are usually included to assist in repairing failed units. However, no provisions are made to contain failures, to gracefully degrade system performance, or to protect other tasks from malfunctioning hardware or software. This is a very common design for dedicated microprocessor systems since it requires no extra hardware or software.

In systems designed for hostile environments, it is assumed that software and hardware may fail in any way, and the system must either continue running or shut itself down in an orderly manner. This type of security design is not common, there being only a handful of expensive commercial or military systems that meet these goals.

A third, and much more common design, is a hybrid of the first two. It is usually found in time sharing systems, and assumes a friendly hardware and system software environment, but a hostile user software environment. In other words, the operating system is assumed to be tested and funtioning correctly, but any user software may be error prone. This is the most common type of security in minicomputers with multiuser or multiprogramming operating systems. Implementation of this security arrangement is normally based on a single hardware memory protection mechanism. Special sets of registers are supplied that contain lower and upper memory addressing limits. These limits are set via **privileged** instructions that may only be executed by the operating system. The limits are enforced by system hardware. During the execution of any one task, these limits assure that the task does not have access to unauthorized memory areas. System security is discussed in more detail in Chapter 11.

Chapter 5

System Support

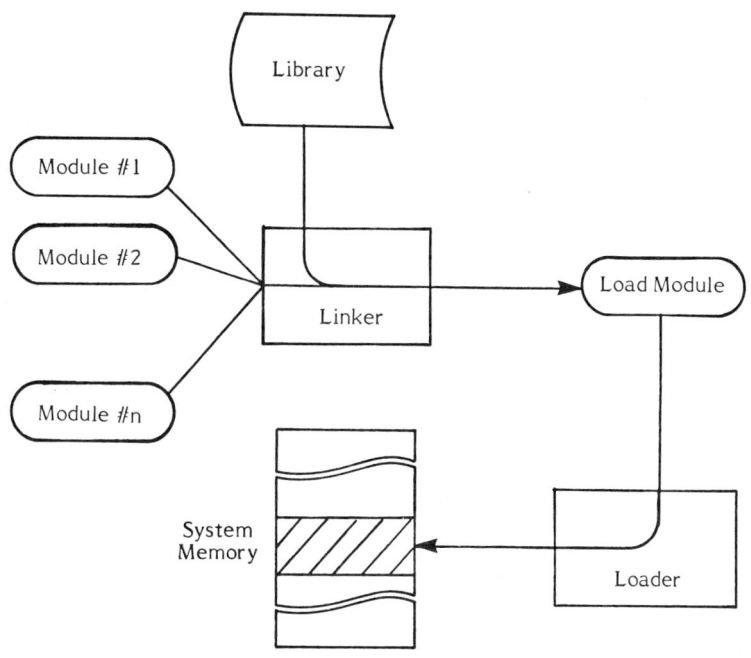

An operating system, besides performing services for tasks as they execute, should assist system users in the design, implementation and testing of new software. The programs and tasks which support software development (called **utilities**) are not usually part of the basic operating system as the system services are. However, they are invaluable in making the computer system easy to use. Not all operating systems provide these utilities - many real time minicomputer and microcomputer applications utilize sophisticated multiprogramming operating systems with no software development utilities. In addition, many cost sensitive system applications do not include these capabilities due to increased memory and peripheral requirements.

System support functions may be divided into the following eight categories:

1) Language Translators
2) Program Editing and Loading
3) Debugging
4) I/O Facilities
5) Libraries
6) System Generation
7) Diagnostics
8) Performance Monitoring

It is interesting to note that a new industry has grown up to support microcomputer system design by providing these utilities in a package called a **microcomputer development system.** This system enables a designer to develop software and hardware as if many of the utilities were present in his final design, but not to incur the costs associated with producing and shipping systems with more resources than needed for the specific application.

Language Translators

Developing new application tasks requires the use of **language translators,** system programs that translate programmer written text into machine executable instructions. Generally, three types of translators are provided with an operating system. The first, and most common, is an **assembler** that produces machine code from a very low level input language. For instance, if the computer architecture provides an instruction which moves the contents of a register to any other register, a typical assembler instruction would be: MOV R2,R5. Writing in assembly language, the programmer has access to all machine instructions. However, along with this unlimited freedom goes the responsibility for determining what registers contain data, saving them when they are used for intermediate calculations, and carefully setting up all data structures. See Figure 5-1 for an example of an assembly language program.

```
LXI   H,X    ; GET ADDRESS OF MAX VALUE
CMP   M      ; COMPARE ACCUMULATOR AGAINST MAX
RNC          ; RETURN IF X > A
MOV   M,A    ; OTHERWISE UPDATE MAX
RET          ; RETURN
```

Figure 5-1   Example of an Assembler Program written in the assembly language for the 8080 microprocessor. This program updates the value stored in memory location X whenever the contents of the accumulator is larger than the previous contents of X.

Interpreters

The second type of language translator is an **interpreter**. The input text to an interpreter is written in a language that is easy to understand, yet powerful and sophisticated. A single command line in this **high level language** (see Figure 5-2) may initiate hundreds of machine operations. Interpreters translate the input text into a set of intermediate instructions for a generalized (or **abstract**) machine. A special program then *interprets* these commands and performs the required functions. In only very

System Support   39

```
10   INPUT S
20   LET X = S * .06
30   LET T = S + X
40   PRINT 'SALES TAX = ',X
50   PRINT 'TOTAL SALE = ',T
60   END
```

Figure 5-2   Example of a BASIC Program which computes 6% sales tax and prints both tax and total sale.

rare instances will these intermediate instructions be directly executable on the processor. This means that interpreters are slower than assembly language programs. On the other hand, since the intermediate instruction set is independent of a particular computer architecture, it is easy to implement a given interpreter on many different machines. Design of the intermediate instruction set must be a careful balance of:

1) Conciseness - The intermediate representation of a program should be considerably shorter than the input text.

2) Functionality - Each intermediate instruction must be easily executed by the interpreting program - the larger the interpreting program, the smaller the user program that can be executed.

3) Power - It must be easy to represent complex data structures and arithmetic operations via the intermediate instruction set.

4) Speed - Since a program is not directly executed on the computer system, an interpreted program is significantly slower than an assembly language program performing the same function due to the overhead involved in interpreting the intermediate instructions.

Interpreters can rival machine code programs on many small microprocessors with very limited instruction sets. Since many of these instruction sets do not have adequate arithmetic (floating point, fixed point integer) and addressing capabilities (indirect, relative, and indexed), code for these processors tends to call subroutines whenever data structures are accessed or when arithmetic computations are to be performed. The system overhead (loading registers, subroutine linkage, etc.) for these operations is very similar to that required for an interpreter. It is generally true that the richer and more powerful the machine instruction set, the larger the speed difference between machine code and interpreted code.

Some well known computer languages which are normally interpreted are APL, PASCAL, BASIC, LISP, and SNOBOL.

Compilers

The third class of language translators contains system programs known as **compilers** that accept input text at a level comparable to that of interpreters. However, these programs translate this text into actual machine instructions. Thus, compiling a program takes considerably longer than translating the program into intermediate code because processor registers must be allocated and the resulting machine code should be optimized. On the other hand, a compiled program usually executes significantly faster than an interpreted program.

It is significantly easier to write programs in a high level language via a compiler than it is to write equivalent assembler programs since a compiler allocates registers automatically, knows when to save them for other calculations, and has predefined data structure access algorithms and subroutine linkage conventions. Thus, the programmer need only worry about the application, and not machine dependent features.

Well known compiled languages are FORTRAN, PL/1, PL/M, COBOL, and ALGOL. A simple FORTRAN program is shown in Figure 5-3.

```
1   FORMAT(F6.2)
2   FORMAT('SALES TAX = ',F6.2)
3   FORMAT('TOTAL SALE = ',F6.2)
    READ(5,1) S
    X = S * .06
    T = S + X
    WRITE(6,2) X
    WRITE(6,3) T
    STOP
    END
```

Figure 5-3   Example of a FORTRAN program which computes 6% sales tax and prints both tax and total sales.

Unique Systems

Some special purpose systems provide interpreters or compilers for company proprietary languages or languages that are unique to a particular application. Process and electrical power control applications often have special languages for implementing control algorithms. In addition to special languages, some machine architectures have been designed or microcoded to directly execute constructs of a high level language. FORTRAN, PASCAL, and COBOL machines are common. These machines are essentially hardware interpreters and therefore can execute intermediate instructions at extremely high speeds.

Program Editing and Loading

In the course of designing and implementing new tasks, programmers require a method by which to enter text and to save it within the system. Facilities must also be provided to easily change this text. Early computer systems utilized decks of specially designed cards which could be generated or modified on a card punch - a typewriter which punched holes in the cards. Almost all modern computer systems provide on-line mass storage devices such as flexible diskettes or hard disk drives on which text may be stored. The **editor**, a system utility, is provided to allow a programmer to create, change, and delete blocks of text on the mass storage devices. Typically, these editors provide powerful, but easy to use, commands that allow searches and substitution of text strings, addition or deletion of text, and movement of text blocks.

When a programmer is satisfied that the stored text is correct, that text is provided as input to one of the system compilers or the assembler. Provided that there are no translation errors, the output of the translator is another block of data that is also stored on the mass storage device. This block of data is referred to as **object code** because it is a representation of machine code that may be directly executed by the processor.

At this point, a system program known as the **linker** is utilized to link all required subroutines and system service calls with the object code to generate a **load module** (a ready to execute task). The load module is then loaded into system memory by the system **loader**. The loader also performs the task of informing the system that the task is in memory and providing any other information required for proper task execution. The link and load sequence is illustrated in Figure 5-4.

Debugging

Debugging is the process of removing errors from software by testing (executing) the software with predetermined data, observing operation, and subsequently changing the software when erroneous operation is noted. It is inherently an iterative process. System software utilities that assist code debugging are often called debuggers.

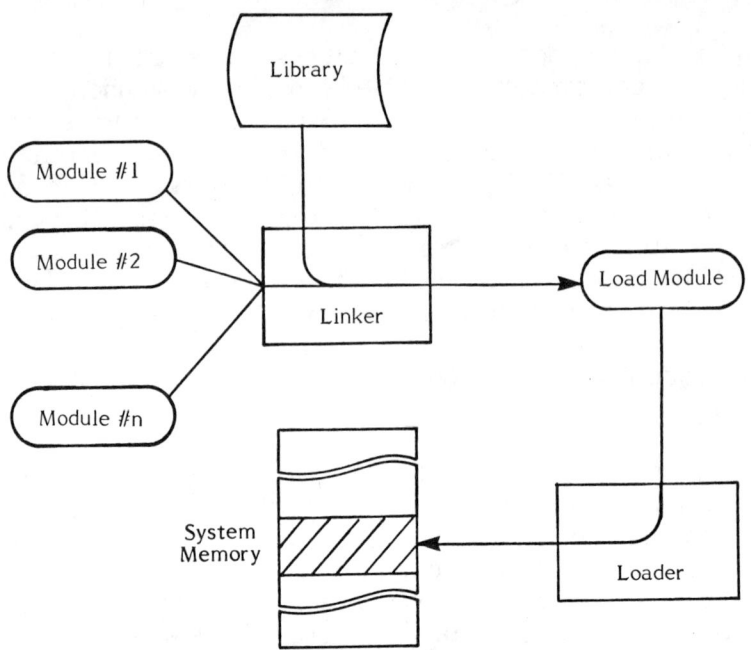

Figure 5-4   User written software modules and required library software are combined into a load module by the linker. The loader is then used to enter the load module into system memory for execution.

Early operating systems supplied a **memory dump** utility that output the contents of system memory on a printer as a response to a program error condition or operator command (see Figure 5-5). The programmer then retired to his office to study the output and to retrace the program's steps until errors were found and corrected.

```
0000    CD 15 E8 3E 1A 06 61 CD 1B E9 04 3D C2 07 E8 CD
0010    62 E9 76 00 00 F5 E5 3E 08 D3 F8 21 C5 CA 22 B6
0020    CA 2A B6 CA 22 C3 CA 21 00 00 22 B8 CA 3E 00 32
0030    CA 32 BC CA 32 BA CA 32 BD CA 06 7C CD 1C EA 01
```

Figure 5-5   Memory Dump Listing. The left column contains the memory address, while the columns to the right display the contents of the next sixteen memory locations in hexadecimal (base 16).

Another debugging support tool is the **trace** utility where each instruction is recorded as it is executed. This record may then be printed as shown in Figure 5-6, and the programmer can recreate the execution of his software. In minicomputer and large time sharing systems, this trace often takes considerably longer than the actual program execution time since each instruction is actually simulated by the trace utility. However, most microcomputer development systems that offer a trace capability perform a limited trace (approximately 100 instructions) in real time through the use of additional processors and high speed memory.

ADDR	INST	A	Z	C
0100	MOV B,A	41	0	1
0101	LDA X	40	0	1
0104	CMP B	40	0	1
0105	RC	40	0	0
0106	MOV M,B	40	0	0
0107	RET	40	0	0

Figure 5-6 A Trace Listing. Each instruction is listed in the order of actual execution. The left column contains the memory address of the instruction; the next column displays the instruction mnemonic. The final columns display the value of the accumulator and flags (Zero, Carry) respectively. When this program was executed, the accumulator contained 41_{16} and the carry flag was set.

While both these methods are extremely useful, they are not sufficient as debugging tools since they tend to waste valuable computer resources and programmer time. Modern **interactive debugging** techniques have mostly supplanted previous off-line methods. These new debugging methods permit a programmer to interact with a task, causing the task to stop and start, examining data structures and register contents, and modifying data where appropriate. In many systems, the programmer may specify that the task is to stop at a predetermined address (called a **breakpoint**) after a specified number of instructions or when a data location is read or written. Using

System Support 45

these facilities, a programmer can find errors and either restart the task or correct the data and proceed to test the next section of code.

Some systems provide an interactive debugging capability known as **symbolic debugging.** This is a very powerful facility where the debugger software has access to program symbol tables that contain names of storage locations and program labels. A programmer may then refer to memory location names rather than absolute addresses. The debugger software performs all computations required to translate a symbol name into the correct memory address. A facility such as this is invaluable with relocatable code or paged systems where code may not be loaded at the same location in memory each time.

Microcomputer development systems offer interactive debugging through a special system interface known as **In Circuit Emulation (ICE).** This facility permits sophisticated debugging software to run in the development system, while a special umbilical cable plugs into the user's prototype hardware system in place of the microprocessor. The programmer can use the debugging capabilities of the development system in conjunction with software and hardware in his prototype system, even if the prototype system has no provisions for debugging software.

I/O Facilities

In addition to providing I/O device driver services to tasks, most operating systems attempt to isolate both users and tasks from the vagaries of individual I/O devices by providing utilities to perform the following functions, independent of the type of peripheral device:

1) **Format** new storage media with system data information so that they may be written and read without error.

2) Display a **directory** of data blocks on any secondary storage media.

3) **Copy** data blocks from one storage device/location to another.

4) **Compress** data on a secondary storage device to reclaim wasted space.

5) **Save** and **restore** data blocks on magnetic tape for backup protection (in the event of system failure) and archival storage.

Libraries

All systems attempt to raise programmer productivity and software reliability. One approach to achieving this goal is to avoid *reinvention of the wheel* by sharing software wherever possible. The ability to establish software **libraries** (collections of program segments which may be used by any task) is a very important feature of any system design. It is the function of the linker to automatically examine specified libraries and to add program segments from the library to the tasks that request them. Libraries frequently contain software for:

1) Floating Point Arithmetic
2) Trigonometric Functions
3) Matrix Arithmetic
4) Linear Programming
5) Curve Fitting
6) Graphics Display Generation
7) Data Formatting
8) Text Editing
9) System Interface

Most systems permit the establishment of multiple libraries so that libraries may be set up for a variety of functions. For example, while compilers such as FORTRAN require some mathematical and data formatting routines found in the FORTRAN library, a particular FORTRAN project may additionally require display generation subroutines found in a special project library. The

System Support 47

linker is usually flexible enough so that it will search multiple libraries in the order specified until it finds the requested software.

System Generation

Most operating systems, while general in nature, must define system parameters which are unique to a specific computer architecture or installation. Examples of these parameters are:

1) System Memory Size - This varies from installation to installation from as little as 4 thousand bytes to more than 4 million bytes.

2) On-Line Disk Storage - Some installations access a single flexible diskette drive while others operate 40 million byte hard disk drives.

3) Number of I/O Devices - Each I/O device requires space in system tables. Systems with only a small amount of memory must keep these system tables as small as possible, while other systems may utilize dozens of peripherals.

4) Buffer Sizes/Buffer Pool - Many systems allocate I/O and message buffers from a fixed memory pool. The size of this area is application dependent and is a tradeoff between system activity and memory size.

Because of installation environment variations, it is often necessary to make modifications to the operating system (as shipped by the supplier) in order to configure it for a particular installation. The process of modifying the operating system is called **system generation** or **SYSGEN** for short. The process of system generation is sometimes a totally manual task of changing code in system routines and then reassembling, linking, and loading the system. This is a very dangerous way of updating an operating system because a variety of undetectable errors may be made, and most installations do not have the expertise to delve into the inner workings of operating system code and data structures.

Modern operating systems normally supply a SYSGEN utility which not only eases the task of modifying an operating system, but also makes it nearly foolproof. It does this by asking questions about the installation interactively through the system console. The answers are checked against known operating system design limits, and the utility builds a new operating system from the data it receives. Another utility is sometimes used to physically move or **install** this new operating system in place of the old.

Diagnostics

Computer systems do not always function correctly; peripheral devices break down and memory errors occur. It is for this reason that most systems are supplied with **diagnostics,** utility programs that attempt to test and isolate faulty areas of the computer system. Diagnostic programs are functionally divided into tests of processor operation and instruction execution, memory, interrupts, timers, terminals, and disk/tape units.

These diagnostic utilities may run in a stand-alone mode or under operating system supervision. Some multiprogramming operating systems permit a peripheral device diagnostic to run at the same time as the normal complement of system tasks. This permits critical computer operations to continue while a peripheral device is under repair - a very important capability in real time process control or communication systems.

System Support. 49

Performance Monitoring

The performance of a loaded operating system is always a critical factor in real time, timesharing, or multiprogramming environments. The only way to compile reliable statistics about system operation is to record data during actual system operation. Good performance monitoring capabilities must be built into the system architecture to do this accurately. For instance, the capability of automatically recording memory accesses and run time for sections of software is a very powerful system capability and permits statistics compilation in a straightforward manner.

Most systems, however, do not include performance monitoring hardware. Some independent firms market add-on hardware that interfaces to existing computer systems, but by far the most usual performance monitoring systems are software based. This software contains timing routines that are called either by the operating system before a task starts and again when it stops, or by special instructions inserted in the task code by a language translator. The operating system timing facility permits monitoring of total task execution time and system overhead, while the language translator facility permits a breakdown of task timing into finer detail (e.g., statistics for each subroutine). These statistics can be extremely useful when attempting to improve overall system performance since the tasks that use the most time can be carefully reworked to increase their speed. Since additional software execution is required for software timing, the system runs somewhat slower overall when this type of performance monitoring is utilized.

Recording system usage information by user or task for accounting or statistics computations is another aspect of performance monitoring common to many operating systems. Users are often billed for processor time, disk storage space, I/O time and terminal connect time based on the **accounting** information recorded by the operating system. This capability is normally found only in large multiuser and batch processing systems.

Chapter 6

Communication and Synchronization

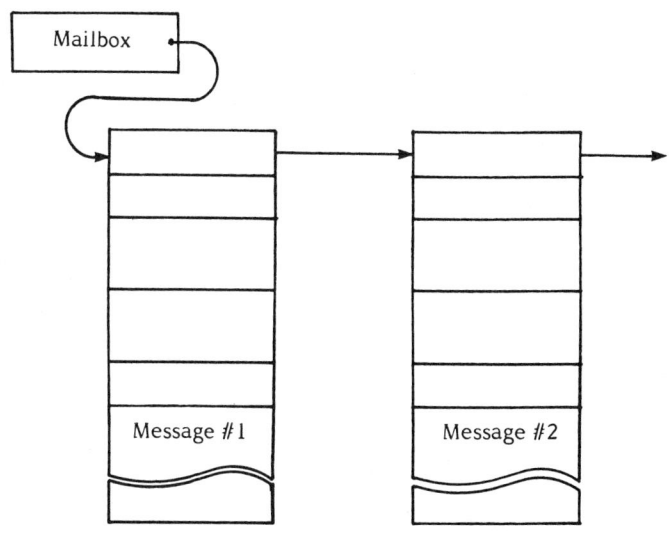

Just as people must communicate with one another in order to get any job done, tasks must also communicate with one another in an operating system environment to coordinate system operation. In general, tasks must communicate to exchange both data and commands. The following are examples of task communication:

1) A program is required to print a message on the console device. It must communicate this message to the console device handler.

2) In a process control system, a high-priority task gathers analog input data whenever an interrupt occurs. This data must then be transferred to a low-priority process in the background which computes standard deviations.

3) A program running under a time sharing operating system requires input from a terminal or multiple terminals. This input must be accepted from the operator any time he depresses a key, even if the program is not yet ready to accept the input (this feature is commonly known as type-ahead). The final line buffer, terminated by a carriage return, must be transmitted to the program when the program is ready to accept it. Sometimes it is necessary to accumulate multiple lines before the program is ready to accept input.

4) A task that could consume a considerable amount of machine time must be executed to complete servicing of an interrupt. Sometimes, a second interrupt will occur before the first interrupt service is complete and the task is ready to accept the next interrupt. Some method of communicating the subsequent interrupt to the service task is required.

Communication

Tasks communicate by exchanging both commands and data. This information may be transmitted through main memory or secondary storage. Sometimes whole data files are transferred from one task to another. This is especially true in real time systems. These blocks of data and commands that are communicated from one task to another are called **messages**.

Messages

The form of a message is different from one operating system to another. Some systems require cooperating tasks to agree to message structure, while others enforce specific protocols. Some systems even allocate memory by way of messages. An example of a message structure is given in Figure 6-1.

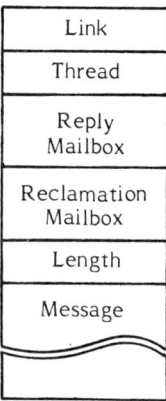

Figure 6-1 Typical Message Format.

A message typically consists of two parts: the message body and the message header. The body of a message contains the command or data information to be transferred between tasks. Most systems permit the size of a message to be variable; message length is then dictated

Communication and Synchronization

only by the quantity of information transmitted. The message header is a section of system information contained within a message consisting of one or more of the following fields:

1) Link - Permits messages to be queued at mailboxes. The queue at a mailbox is often implemented as a **linked list**. The mailbox link points to the first message in the queue and each message points to the message following it in the queue.

2) Thread - Ties all common messages (e.g., I/O buffers) together for system error checking, debugging, or garbage collection.

3) Reply Mailbox - The address of the mailbox to which message replies (acknowledgements) should be sent.

4) Reclamation Mailbox - The address of the mailbox to which messages should be sent when the receiving task has finished processing the message. This mailbox is used by the operating system to reclaim memory space for later reuse.

5) Length - Size of the message body.

Synchronization

In each of the examples at the beginning of this chapter, the data to be transferred between tasks must be transferred when the receiving task is ready for it and must not be allowed to invalidate previously transmitted data. For example, a new message buffer for output must not write over the previous buffer while it is still being printed. This restriction is called **synchronization**. Operating systems solve the synchronization problem in various ways, although all employ primitive synchronizing operations that are included in the kernel.

Event Flag

One technique for synchronization is an **event flag**. This flag is turned on by the transmitting task and turned off by the receiving task. If the flag is off, the transmitting task may send data. After the transfer is complete, the transmitting task turns the flag on. This signals the receiving task to accept the data. When the data has been received and acted upon, the receiving task turns the flag off to permit additional data to be transferred.

This technique is fine for one-way data transfers with a single task transmitting the data. However, multiple tasks are frequently required to communicate with a single task. An example of this is a case where many user tasks must have access to the console logging unit via a console output task or where more than one input task writes numeric data to a shared buffer for statistical calculations. Under these conditions, a simple event flag is not sufficient since there is no easy way to guarantee that only one task accesses the output buffer at a time. A much more general synchronization mechanism is required. Two common mechanisms are **semaphores** and **mailboxes** or **exchanges**.

Semaphores

A semaphore acts like a gate into a restricted area or **critical section** of software (protecting shared data or I/O). Initially the gate is open, but when the first task enters the restricted area, it automatically closes the gate to lock out any other tasks. The task within the critical section may access the shared data with the assurance that no other task will be permitted access until the current task is finished. This locking gate is implemented via two indivisible operations (**P** and **V**). The status of the gate has only two values (*open* or *closed*). When a task wishes access to shared data, it executes a P operation. This operation tests the state of the gate. If the gate is open, it is immediately closed and locked (within the same hardware instruction so that no other task may interrupt this *test and set* operation). If the gate is closed, the task may not enter the critical section and it must wait until the gate is reopened.

Once a task has gained access to shared data via the P operation, it performs the required data manipulation and exits the critical section. At this point the task executes the V operation that opens the gate and allows one and only one of the waiting tasks to enter the section. If no tasks are waiting, the gate is left open for the next task that wishes access.

Busy Wait

The only problem posed by semaphores occurs when they are totally implemented in software since in order to enter the critical region, a test of the "gate" must be made to determine whether it is open or closed. If it is closed, a task must wait until it is opened. Unless there is some hardware facility for waiting, the task must continually test this gate. Even though the task is not performing any useful work during the wait, the processor that the task is running on is busy executing test instructions which prevent any other task from executing during this time. This is called a **busy wait**.

Mailboxes

Mailboxes are a slightly different method of implementing task synchronization. When a task has data to send to another cooperating task, it places a message containing the data in a mailbox for the receiving task. This mailbox is actually a **queue** where messages are stacked up, and the receiving task, when it is ready, looks in the mailbox and picks up the next message. Any number of transmitting tasks can place messages in the mailbox. In order to make mailboxes work correctly, three indivisible operations must be defined:

1) **send** - places a message in the appropriate mailbox.

2) **wait** - extracts a message from the appropriate mailbox. It will wait until a message arrives if the mailbox is empty. The task is suspended during this time.

3) **accept** - extracts a message from the appropriate mailbox, but does not wait if the mailbox is empty. This permits tasks to check multiple mailboxes periodically for messages.

It should be noted that when mailboxes are used, an inherent critical section is contained in the code which implements the queue operations. It is imperative that an addition to or a removal from the queue is protected by a semaphore until the operation completes. Some machines have hardware to assure this. However, all queue operations generally involve the execution of multiple instructions.

Some operating systems force all synchronization operations to occur at interrupts and coordinate these operations with the scheduler. In this case, a timer is usually dedicated to system interrupts to guarantee service to all tasks. Whenever an interrupt occurs, tasks are examined in order of priority (see Chapter 7) to determine which should be executed. For example, if a task was waiting at a mailbox, it will become ready to run (eligible for scheduling) when a message is received at the mailbox.

Chapter 7

Scheduling

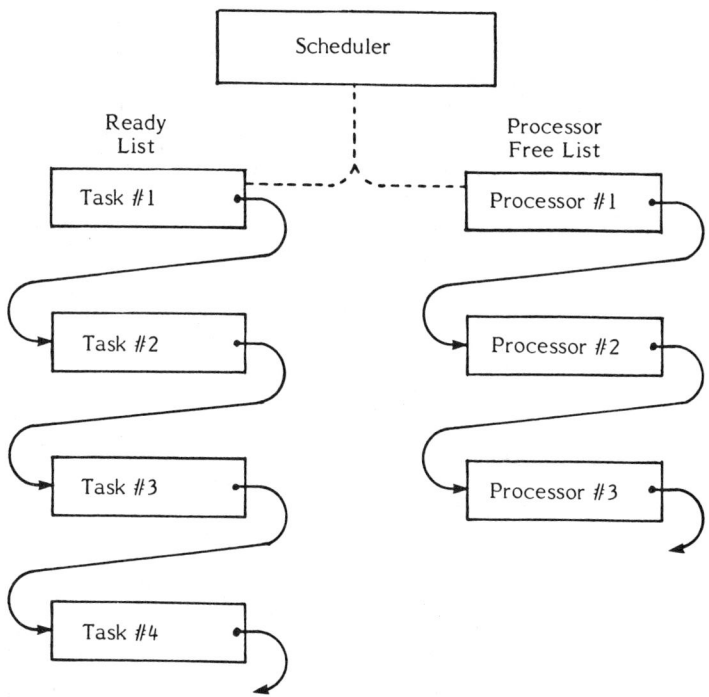

The **scheduler** or **dispatcher** is the heart of the operating system. It ensures that the right tasks execute at the right times in order to guarantee reliable and efficient system performance. The scheduler is the portion of the kernel system software that enforces rules (commonly called scheduling algorithms) to determine which task within the Ready List should be executed next.

Generally the scheduler operates whenever a task stops executing. In systems utilizing **non-preemptive** scheduling techniques, a task stops executing only when it is complete. This type of scheduling is common in batch systems. **Preemptive** scheduling methods on the other hand, permit tasks to voluntarily stop executing while waiting for an event (interrupt, message, or completion of an I/O transfer) and allow the operating system to force tasks to stop executing when a more important task (e.g., power down) must be executed. Preemptive scheduling is used in multiprogramming and real time operating systems.

Queueing theory, simulation, and peformance monitoring have all been used extensively in the development of scheduling strategies. In many systems it is possible to statistically predict the frequency, size, and resource requirements of the programs that execute on the system. With this information, the average number of tasks waiting to execute and the average length of the wait may be computed and used to compare scheduling strategies. Readers interested in formal treatment of the subject are referred to the volumes listed in Appendix B.

Non-Preemptive Scheduling

Non-preemptive scheduling requires that a task run to completion once it begins executing. The scheduler must predict task requirements and attempt to execute these tasks in a manner that minimizes turn-around time. Since the scheduler cannot stop tasks once they are executing, the resources (maximum processor time, memory, and peripheral devices) needed by the task must be specified by the user before the task is executed. The most simple type of non-preemptive scheduling algorithm is **FIFO** or first-in first-out scheduling. This algorithm operates by treating the Ready List as a queue (like a checkout line in a supermarket). The next task to execute is always the first in the queue (the task that has been waiting the longest). FIFO strategies are not usually adequate when both large and small tasks are executed on the same system.

To keep average turn-around time short, an algorithm is often implemented where the next task selected to execute is the smallest (lowest predicted execution time and lowest memory requirement) in the Ready List. In order to prevent a user from understating the requirements of a task in order to make it execute faster, most systems automatically abort task execution if the predefined limits are exceeded. The major deficiency of this algorithm is the possibility of completely locking out large tasks because there are always small tasks in the Ready List. This is avoided by permitting large jobs to begin execution after they've been waiting in the Ready List for a long period of time.

Preemptive Scheduling

The next step in scheduling complexity is called **priority** or **preemptive scheduling**. To implement this scheduling algorithm, each task is given an execution priority. Generally, the higher the task priority, the more important it is for the task to be executed. If task priorities are fixed, they are called **static priorities**. **Dynamic priorities**, on the other hand, may be changed by system software due to changing conditions. Preemptive scheduling can only be implemented in multiprogramming systems where tasks may be suspended and restarted.

The simplest type of preemptive scheduling algorithm is called **round-robin** scheduling. Using this algorithm, each task in the Ready List is executed in order. In the simplest case, each task, once started, executes until it is suspended to wait for an event or to permit a higher priority task to execute. The scheduler then starts execution of the next task on the Ready List.

This basic scheduling concept can be expanded to include **time sharing** facilities in which each task, when executed, is given a maximum execution time limit called a **time slice**. Time slices are on the order of 1 to 50 milliseconds. If a task has not completed execution and has not exited to the scheduler within this time limit, the task's execution is interrupted, its context is saved, it is placed back on the Ready List, and the scheduler determines the next task to execute. This time slice is physically enforced via an **interval timer** or **real time clock**. The timer is started when task execution is started and, if the scheduler has not started executing before the time slice expires, an interrupt is generated that causes the current task to stop executing.

This type of scheduling algorithm ensures that no task can monopolize the processor and that the tasks will be executed in order - thus the term round-robin. The time sharing facility is especially important on a large computer system where, after typing a command, each user expects the system to respond within a short period of time. This period is commonly referred to as the **response time**. Systems are usually designed to guarantee between 1 and 2 second response times.

Preemptive schedulers are usually set up so that the scheduling algorithm is run whenever an event occurs. An event that causes execution of the scheduler can be a hardware interrupt from an I/O device, a system interval timer, or another processor or it can be a voluntary or forced task suspension while a requested operation is completed. Since tasks may be waiting on this event, the first function of the scheduler is to examine suspended tasks and move those waiting on this event to the Ready List. Then, the highest priority task is extracted from the Ready List, its context is restored if required, and it is executed. In practice, the Ready List tasks are ordered with respect to priority so that the first task on the list is the highest priority.

Some operating systems assign priority on a dynamic basis where a task entering the system is given a basic priority that has either been defined by the console operator or computed from run time, memory requirements, resource utilization, and I/O predictions. As a task waits in the Ready List, its priority is increased in proportion to the time it has been waiting. Thus, even if many high-priority tasks are executing, after sufficient time the low-priority task will have attained a high enough priority to guarantee a time slice. This is a particularly useful facility in large time sharing systems where small tasks are given high-priority. During busy times of the day, so many small tasks are waiting for execution that low-priority tasks may never execute if they rely solely on static priority.

Foreground/background systems utilize a dual scheduling strategy. The foreground operates on a priority basis while the background operates in a non-preemptive mode with a FIFO strategy. Tasks in the foreground always preempt tasks in the background.

Overhead Reduction

One other interesting scheduling technique is that of lowering the priority of a program based on the length of time it has been executing and at the same time increasing the length of the time slice during which it may execute. This method is useful in demand paging or swapping systems where a large overhead penalty is paid whenever a job is moved between the Running and Suspended task states. This strategy utilizes the past history of a task to permit it to achieve the same amount of computation with less system overhead.

Most microprocessor and real time minicomputer systems keep tasks in system memory at all times to reduce task state transition overhead. Larger and more sophisticated systems attempt to achieve the same end by keeping some dedicated tasks (I/O drivers, file editors) in memory and by requiring that all system tasks (assemblers, compilers, and editors) be reentrant. When tasks are reentrant, the same physical code may be shared by more than one user, thereby reducing system memory requirements.

Chapter 8

Resource and Memory Management

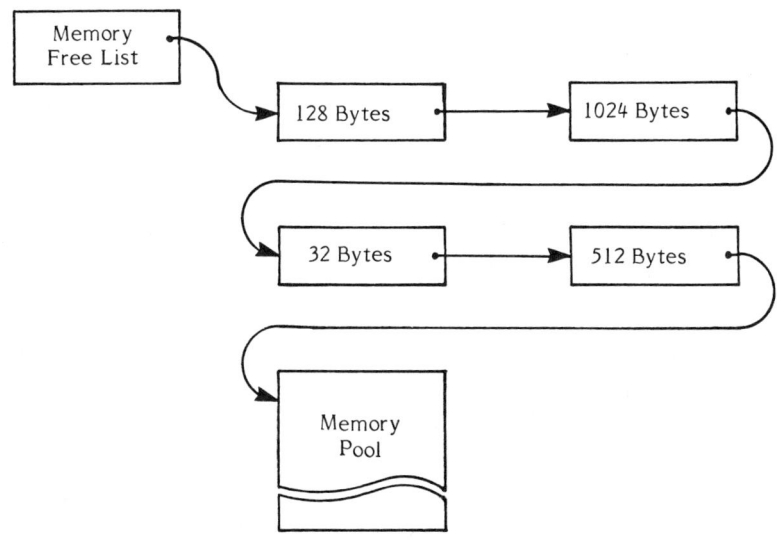

Computer system assets such as memory space, disk files, peripheral devices, and even processors in a multiprocessing system, are known as **resources**. Tasks utilize system resources in order to perform their functions. For example, an alarm logging task must print alarms on the system console, while the assembler task must read source text from a disk file and write the resulting object code to another file. The system console and disk files are resources. Since there invariably are more tasks in a system than resources to support all of them simultaneously, a strategy must be implemented by which the interaction between the finite resource base and the tasks that require their use is managed. This is the responsibility of the operating system.

Consumable and Reusable Resources

System resources may be divided into two classes: **consumable resources** and **serially reusable resources**. A consumable resource is produced by one task (known as the **producer**) and consumed by another task (known as the **consumer**). For example, message information is packed in memory locations allocated to the producer by the operating system. The message is then sent to another task where it is consumed (read and acted on). The receiving task then discards the packing material (memory) by releasing it back to the memory manager. Consumable resources generally have a short lifetime with respect to the lifetime of a task.

Resources that can normally be used by only one task at a time, but can be reused later by other tasks, are appropriately known as serially reusable resources. Printers, terminals, disk files, and tape units are serially reusable resources. To use these resources, a task must request the resource, wait for the resource to be allocated, use the resource, and finally release the resource back to the operating system.

Resource Management

The critical aspects of both resource and memory management are extremely similar from the point of view of a task requiring either type of resource to perform its specific function. However, some operating systems require that memory management functions allocate memory for tasks as they move from one task state to another. Since all tasks require residence in system memory in order to execute, the memory manager must ensure that a task entering the running state is moved (if necessary) from secondary storage. In some cases, this means that suspended tasks will be swapped out to secondary storage in order to create room for the running task. The following discussion will be limited to discussing memory management only as it applies to consumable resources.

A task requests a resource via the **assign** system service. If there are no resources available, the task waits until the resource becomes available. The resource is then assigned exclusively to the requesting task that proceeds to use it as required. When the task no longer needs to use the resource, the **release** service is utilized to return the resource to the operating system which then assigns the resource to the next requesting task. In some systems, the console device is treated in a slightly more involved manner by defining a system task for the console interface. This task assigns the console forever, and user tasks send print request messages to the console interface task. In real time systems, this feature permits high-priority alarm messages to be displayed and printed even though another task may be printing a lengthy report.

Secondary storage management is treated in detail in Chapter 10.

Memory for consumable resources such as messages and I/O buffers is managed in the same manner as printers and terminals by the system services **allocate** (to assign a block of memory) and **free** (to release memory). However,

Resource and Memory Management   67

since the size of the memory resource required by a task may vary with the application, a somewhat more flexible technique must be utilized for dispensing and reclaiming this resource. Often, memory areas called **pools** are set aside at SYSGEN time and are used by the memory manager to supply memory blocks to tasks for specific purposes. For example, a buffer pool may be set aside to provide I/O buffers for interface to peripheral devices. Initially, a pool begins as a contiguous memory area. The memory manager allocates memory to a task by removing a block of the required size from the pool and informing the requesting task of its position. Some systems add a message header to the allocated memory and actually send the block as a message to the requesting task that is then free to use the memory as required.

As memory blocks are returned to the memory manager, a list of free blocks is built (Figure 8-1). Additional memory requests cause the memory manager to first examine this list to determine if one of the returned blocks satisfies the request before removing memory from the remaining pool. Two strategies may be used to allocate the requested

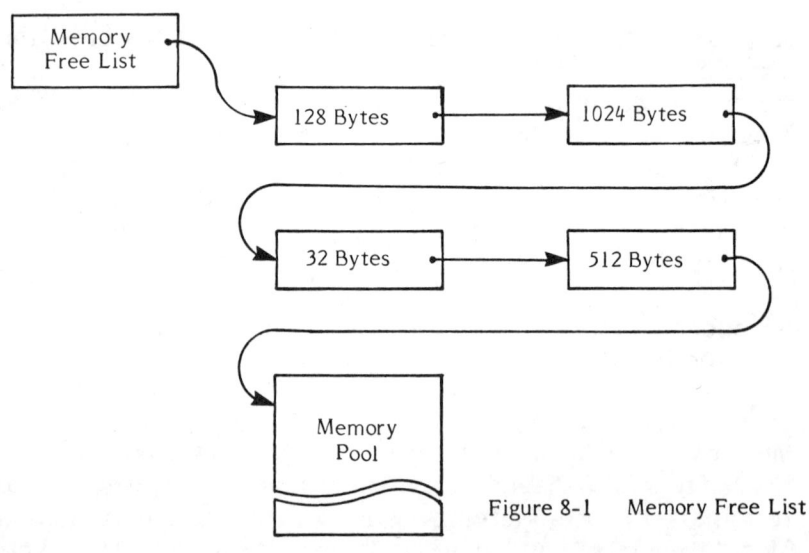

Figure 8-1   Memory Free List

memory from available blocks. The simplest is known as **first fit**, where the first block large enough to satisfy the request is used for allocation. The second method, **best fit**, finds an available memory block that is very close in size to the requested block. Referring to Figure 8-1, a task requesting 30 bytes would be allocated memory from the 128 byte area using the first fit method and from the 32 byte area with the best fit method. Intuitively, the best fit algorithm seems superior since it wastes the least amount of memory during allocation, although it is the slower of the two strategies. However, simulations have determined that the first fit strategy is simpler and leads to less memory fragmentation.

Often, the memory manager is designed in such a way that if a returned block is adjacent to a block already in the free list, the two blocks are joined into a single block. This larger block usually provides more allocation flexibility than two small blocks. If blocks are not automatically joined when they are returned, large memory blocks tend to be continuously broken into smaller pieces since small messages are much more common than large buffers. This may lead to a condition known as **fragmentation** where leftover sections of memory are too small to fill an allocation request. When this happens and a request is made for a contiguous block larger than those on the list, the memory manager must perform **garbage collection** on the free list. This is usually a time consuming function whereby the free list is scanned from beginning to end and all contiguous memory blocks are concatenated. If this yields a block large enough to satisfy the request, it is allocated to the task; otherwise the task must wait until more blocks are freed.

As you can see, the memory management problem is significantly easier when buffers and/or messages allocated from a single pool are all the same size. The system may then treat the pool as a fixed list of buffers and fragmentation (and the resulting garbage collection) never occurs.

Resource and Memory Management

Memory Management

General memory management (as opposed to the allocation of buffer pools) is closely related to the process of scheduling, and a great deal of work has been done on techniques for managing the memory resource. All tasks require system memory in order to run, and traditionally this memory has been extremely expensive. Even with prices dropping very rapidly, it is still considerably more expensive than secondary storage. Thus, effective memory management will continue to play a key role in operating system designs. Memory management directly related to running a task is normally a system function that is invisible to the task being executed. When the scheduler extracts a task from the Ready List for execution, the task must be loaded into system memory if it does not currently reside there. The system architecture determines how much of the task must be in memory before execution of the task may begin. Some systems require loading of the complete task, while others require only that the currently executing instruction be memory resident.

Most real time minicomputer and microcomputer systems require that tasks reside and remain in dedicated memory areas so no loading is required. In fact, many microcomputer systems are designed so that all tasks are ROM resident.

Segmentation

Implementation of management strategies that do not require a complete task to be resident in memory is generally based on dividing a task into **segments** and/or **pages**. A segment is an arbitrary user-defined block of data or instructions that functions as an independent unit. A task may be composed of many segments, large or small. Systems may reference segments by names or numbers. Named references require a **content-addressable memory;** otherwise a segment table search would be required for every memory access. Segment locations in memory may be fixed by a language translator, by the linker, or by the loader. With fixed locations, a task cannot be dynamically relocated while it is executing; it must always occupy the same memory locations whenever it executes.

Most machines with large address spaces perform segmentation by utilizing a flexible device called a **base register**. When a task is executing, the base register is set by the operating system to the physical address of the first instruction or data byte of the segment. All references within a segment are addressed relative to the base address of the segment. Then, during execution, the base register contents are added to the relative addresses to form the actual physical address. If the segment is moved in memory for any reason, execution may be easily continued by simply resetting the base register contents. The number of segments active at any one time depends on the number of base registers. Some systems contain only two segments (one for code and one for data), while others utilize a segment table where any number or segments and their base addresses may be listed for a given task. However, in order to speed execution time, these general segment-table systems always contain a small content-addressable memory of recently-used segment base addresses so that the system does not normally waste an extra memory access for each data or instruction access. Base register or segment table contents must be saved as part of the task context when task execution is suspended.

In a segmented system, an executing task must have its executing segment in memory. Since segment sizes are arbitrary, a fixed memory space must be filled with variable sized segments. The algorithms for allocation control are identical to those described previously for memory pools.

Utilizing the concept of a segment and base register, memory protection can be easily implemented by associating a **length register** with each segment. Then, any physical memory access below the base register or above the base register plus the length register (see Figure 8-2) is trapped as a **protection violation**.

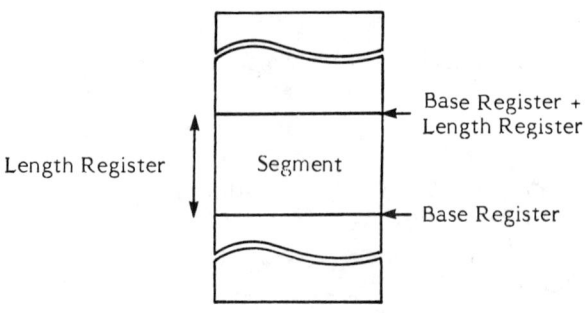

Figure 8-2   Segment Memory Limits used for Memory Protection.

Paging

A further refinement of the segmentation technique divides each segment into a number of **pages** that are normally fixed-size blocks between 512 bytes and 4096 bytes in length. Whether pages are of fixed or variable size, memory fragmentation occurs. With fixed-size pages, the last page of a segment is usually only partially filled, whereas variable-sized pages never fit neatly into a given memory area and cause wasted space between pages. Fragmentation due to a fixed page size is, however, somewhat easier to handle.

In a paging system, each segment has a page table associated with it, and each page number is looked up in the page table for each memory access. In practice most paging systems use a small, high speed content-addressable memory to store page addresses in order to avoid the extra memory accesses required to look up pages in the page table. If the page is currently in memory, the physical address of the reference is computed from the information in the page table. If the page is not available in memory, it must be fetched from secondary storage. This condition is known as a **page fault** and causes the currently executing task to be suspended. After the required page is loaded, execution may continue. This technique is known as **demand paging**. When a page is to be moved into memory from secondary storage, it is likely that some other page must be removed to make room for it. Three page-replacement strategies are common:

1) Random - A page is picked at random for removal. This, on occasion, may be a page required to continue execution.

2) First-In First-Out - The oldest page in memory is selected for replacement. This technique assumes that the least likely page to be used in the future is the page that has been in memory the longest.

3) Least Recently Used - The page selected for replacement is the one that has been unused for the longest time. This strategy assumes that pages which are unused for long periods of time are least likely to be used in the future.

Virtual Memory

The level of memory management previously described permits tasks to be written and executed without the need to worry about memory allocation strategies. The next logical step is to completely divorce the **physical address** space (actual memory) from the **logical address** space (the memory that a task addresses when it executes). This technique, **virtual memory,** permits programs to be written independently of the physical system memory available. Thus, programmers may build programs which are considerably larger than the available physical memory space without the need for **overlays.** Because the logical address space is very large (typically between 16 million and 4 billion bytes) and the number of segments is not

Resource and Memory Management 73

limited, **associative memory** must be utilized for page/ segment access via the page and segment tables, respectively. If associative memory were not used, each memory access would require a segment table access followed by a page table access just to compute the physical memory address.

Virtual memory implementations usually provide an additional benefit to programmers by allowing secondary storage files to be **attached** to a task and thereafter utilized as if they were task segments. This means that a program can perform normal memory reads and writes to the file, and no special I/O coding or buffers need to be used.

Deadlocks

Any occurrence that limits the efficiency of a computer system or causes tasks to be suspended indefinitely is a dangerous circumstance. Two such problems are resource **deadlocks** and **thrashing**. Deadlocks are caused when tasks reach an impasse in resource allocation where no task may continue because it needs a resource that another task possesses. If other tasks cannot release their resources until they are allocated additional resources, a "catch 22" situation exists where no task can continue until another task continues. The following examples show how easy it is to enter a deadlock situation:

1) A system contains two tasks (A and B) and two cassette tape units (T1 and T2). Task A assigns tape unit T1 and begins to read. While waiting for data, the operating system permits task B to assign tape unit T2 and to begin reading data. After a short computation, task A requires another tape unit to write results on. Since T2 is still assigned, task A is suspended and task B continues. After a time, task B requires another tape unit for data output. However, since T1 is still assigned, task B is now suspended. At this time, neither task can

run until a tape unit is released, and a tape unit can't be released until one of the tasks runs.

2) A multiprogramming operating system is designed so that tasks communicate via messages. Transmitting tasks request message buffers from a single buffer pool, and receiving tasks return completed messages to the pool for reuse. If one task fails to return messages to the pool, the message buffer pool will shrink each time the task receives a message. Finally, no messages will be available, and every task will eventually enter the suspended state.

Deadlocks are difficult to correct and even more difficult to predict. In order to remove a deadlock, the system generally must start destroying tasks and reclaiming their resources until enough resources are available to permit one of the suspended tasks to resume execution. It is best to avoid this situation entirely. This is easy when designing dedicated systems since each task function can be implemented in such a way as to prevent deadlock situations from occurring. On general purpose (especially time sharing) systems, it is impossible to prevent deadlocks unless each task is required to inform the system in advance of resource requirements. The operating system can then implement global strategies that will not permit tasks to begin execution if potential deadlock situations exist.

Readers interested in a formal treatment of deadlock avoidance and recovery are referred to the volumes listed in Appendix B.

Thrashing

Paging systems require considerable system overhead for servicing page faults. If a large number of programs are

Resource and Memory Management 75

executing (as with a large number of users in a time sharing system environment), a point can be reached where page faults occur so often that system efficiency is drastically degraded. This state is known as thrashing, as the system is literally flailing away at moving pages to and from secondary storage. This condition can become so extreme that system overhead approaches 100% of total system availability and no useful work is accomplished while the operating system spends all its time servicing page faults and executing replacement algorithms.

This problem has received much attention in the literature. So far, the best approach to avoiding the thrashing condition has been by making use of the **working set** concept. A task working set is the set of pages that a given task references in a specified period of time. The size of this set may be approximated for any task by measuring it from time to time and assuming that the size of the working set changes slowly with respect to time. Thus, thrashing may be avoided if a task is only loaded for execution when the operating system has determined that there are sufficient free pages in memory to contain the task working set without disrupting other tasks.

Chapter 9

Input and Output

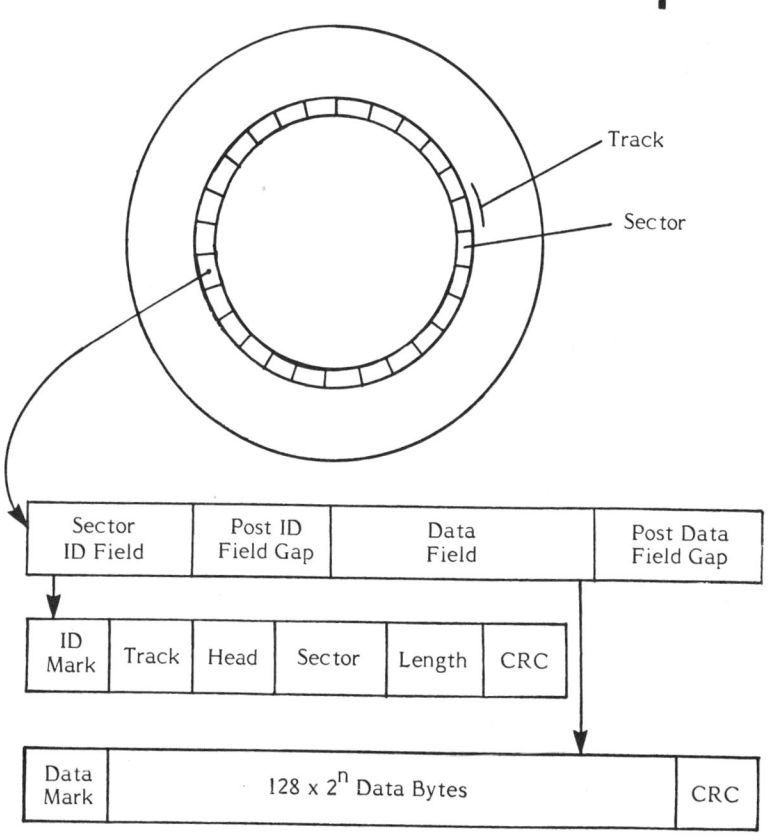

The wide variety of input and output devices makes it almost impossible for each programmer to design and implement all the tasks necessary to interface with them. Therefore, operating systems supply a set of tasks called **device drivers**, each of which contains the necessary software to receive data from, or transmit data to, peripherals. Many operating systems, especially those used with microcomputers, also include the capability to add custom device drivers for hardware that is unique to a given installation.

Device drivers normally have a standard interface to the operating system through which they service interrupts and pass transmitted and received data.

I/O Architecture

Device drivers may support various types of I/O architectures depending on the system design. Generally, there are two classes of I/O architecture, **direct I/O** and **indirect I/O**. Direct I/O is a technique where a processor directly accesses an I/O port with an input or output instruction. Most basic microprocessor systems utilize this facility, and most microprocessors have a set of I/O instructions. Direct I/O may be **memory mapped** or **I/O mapped**. Input or output transfers that are accomplished by accessing I/O ports with special *INPUT* or *OUTPUT* instructions are said to be I/O mapped. I/O mapping requires separate address decoding for memory and I/O transfers.

Memory mapping provides I/O ports which are addressed as if they were memory locations. However, memory mapping does not imply that all memory operations (e.g., increment memory) may be performed on a memory mapped I/O port. This is due to the fact that some peripheral control registers may be either *read only* or *write only*. In fact, some hardware designs mate write only control data with read only status data in order to save memory addresses. Thus, writes and reads of the same memory location may have no relation to one another.

Examples of both types of direct I/O implementations may be easily found in contemporary systems.

When input and output operations are controlled by an independent processing unit, it is called indirect I/O. This processing unit is known as an I/O channel or I/O processor and is normally exclusively dedicated to I/O transfers. Often the instruction set of an I/O processor is oriented solely to I/O functions and it cannot function as a general purpose processor. An I/O processor can execute in parallel with a general purpose processor. However, all system processors normally share the same memory via one of the following four methods:

1) **DMA** - The processor is placed in a wait mode (usually called HOLD in microprocessor systems), while the I/O processor transfers data to or from memory at the maximum memory data rate. When the data transfer is complete, the processor resumes execution.

2) **Cycle Stealing** - Since memory cycle time is significantly shorter than processor cycle time, the I/O processor synchronizes with the general processor and steals memory cycles for data transfers between the memory cycles used by the general processor.

3) **Dual Port Memory** - If system memory units are designed with two complete data paths, both the general processor and the I/O processor may request memory cycles asynchronously. Since the memory can only perform one function at a time, dual port arbitration logic is designed to permit access on a first-come, first-served basis, with one port (usually the general processor) having priority for simultaneous requests.

4) **Buffer Memory** - The I/O processor may have a small high-speed memory buffer locally

Input and Output

accessible where it temporarily stores data from very high-speed devices (such as fixed head disks or bubble memories) until it can acquire a data path to memory via one of the three previous methods.

I/O Subsystems

Once device drivers have been incorporated into an operating system, the next logical step is the construction of a subsystem that performs input and output for requesting tasks. Subsystems such as these are known as **I/O executives, I/O supervisors,** or **I/O subsystems.** These subsystems improve programmer efficiency and conserve runtime storage because the I/O functions are designed, implemented, and loaded only once for an operating system. A typical I/O subsystem contains device drivers, performs I/O buffer administration, handles error conditions, and provides a uniform interfacing structure through which tasks may request I/O transfers.

The I/O subsystem masks the vagaries of various I/O devices by permitting a task to reference devices via a **logical device** designation. This means that a device may be referred to by a name or number, without knowing in advance whether the device is a card reader, tape drive, or disk file. At execution time, the operator, or another task, may assign **physical devices** to the logical designations. With this assignment, the I/O subsystem ensures that the proper device drivers are utilized to perform the I/O transfers. An example of the power of this technique is an Assembler task that reads data from the logical input device "IN" and subsequently writes the object code to the logical output device "OUT". A simple assignment, with no change to the Assembler task, then permits input to be accepted from the card reader or a disk file. In the same manner, object code output may be directed to another disk file, to the card punch, or to the paper tape punch.

The I/O subsystem also manages I/O resources. This function embodies two basic activities: buffer administration and device allocation. Buffer administration involves allocating memory areas for data transfers and reclaiming used areas. Buffer memory allocation techniques are described in Chapter 8. Device allocation, which deals with the ability to grant a task exclusive use of a resource and still maintain system efficiency, is also discussed in Chapter 8.

I/O devices (especially mass storage devices) have **soft error** rates that are considerably higher than their **hard error** rates. A soft error is a dynamic error normally caused by some transient condition, while a hard error is a repeatable error in the magnetic media or electronics. Data transfer errors are generally fielded by the I/O subsystem. Several attempts or **retries** at an I/O transfer are usually made before declaring a failure. Some systems rely on **error codes** (e.g., **checksums**) in order to assure data integrity, while others actually sacrifice system performance by automatically performing a read-after-write check against the transferred data.

In systems containing an I/O processor, the I/O subsystem often builds lists consisting of multiple I/O requests. These lists are automatically executed in series by the I/O processor. This is known as **chaining**. I/O processors pose problems in paged systems due to the fact that they often lack the addressing modes of the general system processor. For instance, some systems with base registers require all I/O functions to operate with absolute physical addresses. This means that a segment/page waiting for I/O may not be removed from, or relocated, in system memory since if it was replaced by another segment, the I/O operation would cause a protection violation. I/O processors with system memory addressing modes identical to the general processor do not require these special operating restrictions.

Input and Output

Spooling

In order to improve system efficiency, many I/O subsystems queue I/O transfers to a device that is currently busy. This capability is most often used in conjunction with system printers. Thus, to print data, a task actually writes the data to a disk file that is assigned to take the place of the printer. When the task completes its writing, the disk file is automatically entered into the print queue and is eventually printed on the system printer. The program that manages the queues and the appropriate I/O devices is called a **spooler**. Additionally, operator commands are usually provided to rearrange the queue or to delete print requests.

Chapter 10

File Systems

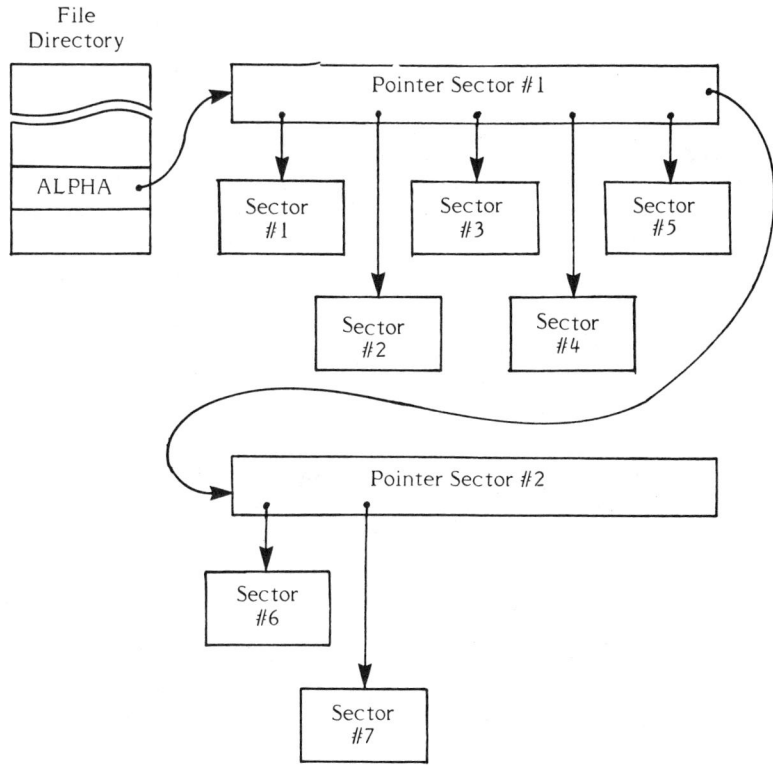

As discussed in the previous chapter, tasks input and output data via the peripheral devices designed into the computer system. In addition to logging messages on the console, reading programs from the card reader, and accepting programmer input from a terminal, tasks require the ability to store large amounts of data for reference at some future time. For example, commonly used programs, source text, intermediate calculations and data bases (such as payroll information) are stored, moved, and updated by both programmers and tasks within the system. The **File System** provides these capabilities. Modern secondary storage devices contain large amounts of low cost storage (between 1 and 300 million bytes). The file system partitions this storage into smaller areas, called files, that can be utilized by tasks for data and program storage.

Media

The media normally associated with file systems are disk and tape drives, CCD storage units, and bubble memory devices. Disk drives often are further subdivided into fixed-head disks (or drums) and moving-head disks. Fixed-head disks have considerably faster access times than moving head disks, but have smaller storage capacities. CCD and bubble memory devices offer even higher speeds and ease of use when compared to disk technology, but are higher in cost.

Speeds and cost vary drastically among the above storage device types as follows:

1) Fixed-Head Disk, CCD, Bubble Memory - High speed and high cost; effective as a swapping or paging store or where buffering of lower speed disk devices is required; access time varies from 125 microseconds for CCD to 8 milliseconds for fixed head disk.

2) Moving-Head Disk - General all-around work horse of the mass storage industry; low cost; access times vary from 40 milliseconds for a rigid disk to 300 milliseconds for a flexible diskette.

3) Tape - Extremely low cost and low speed; usually used only for large data bases or as archival storage. Access times for large tapes may be as long as 30 minutes.

It is interesting to note that bubble memory storage is equivalent to an inertia-less fixed-head disk. Where a fixed head disk must constantly rotate, bubble devices may be started and stopped at will. Initial positioning to a random data record by either device requires approximately the same access time. However, subsequent sequential data transfers require no additional access time with bubble memories.

Media Organization

New media must usually be written with a fixed **format** by the system hardware/software before it is used to store data. Formatting is a method of taking raw media and adding the necessary information to permit the system to read and write data without error. This format may contain moving head servo and addressing information. Disks and drums are usually divided into **tracks** and **sectors**. A track is the area covered by a stationary read/write head with one revolution of the media. The amount of information stored on a track is a function of the recording density and the size of the track. For instance, IBM soft-sectored single density flexible diskettes store 3328 bytes per track.

A sector is an arbitrary division of a track. Many sectors may be included on a single track, depending on track and sector sizes. Normally sectors are all the same size. IBM soft-sectored single density flexible diskettes typically

File Systems 85

allocate 26 sectors to a track with each sector consisting of 128 bytes. Depending on the physical device, sector sizes may be as large as four thousand bytes. In a paging system, the page size should be a multiple of the sector size in order to ease the I/O overhead. Figure 10-1 gives an example of the IBM soft-sectored single density flexible disk format.

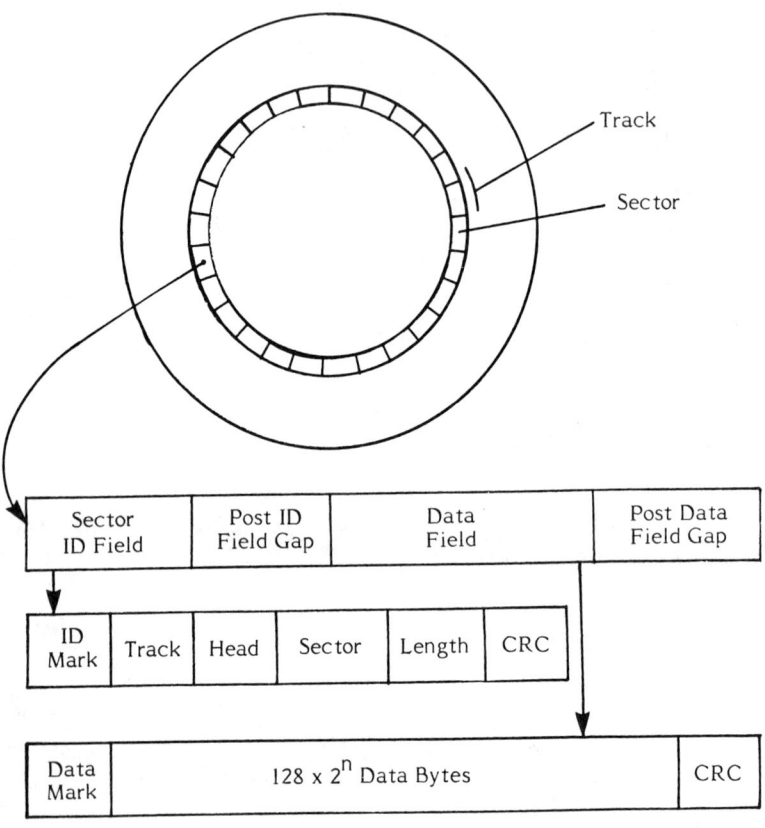

Figure 10-1   IBM Soft Sectored Single Density Flexible Diskette Format.

The initial formatting of a disk determines where sectors are located within a track. Some systems simply allocate sectors sequentially. However, when multiple sectors are to be read or written, disk rotational timing is critical.

OPERATING SYSTEMS

For instance, when the first sector has been read, the processor may begin another transfer for the next sector. Since the disk has continued to rotate, the next sector on the disk is already passing under the read/write head, and the processor must wait for another complete revolution of the disk (40-100 milliseconds) before the data may actually be input. To improve performance, a technique known as **interleaving** is utilized. Thus, sectors are not stored sequentially within a track, but physically removed from the previous sector by some number (known as the **interleave factor**) of physical sectors as shown in Figure 10-2.

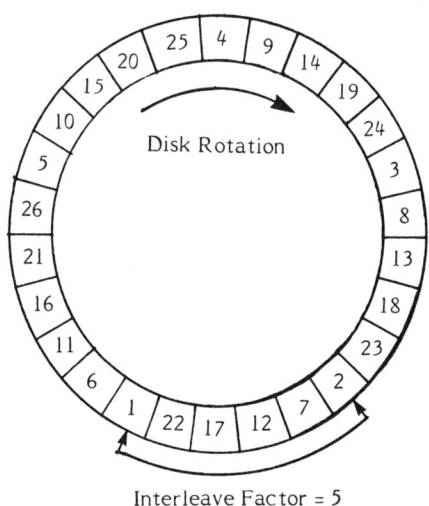

Interleave Factor = 5

Figure 10-2 Interleaved Sector Allocation Within a Track.

Tapes are simply treated as a series of fixed size data blocks, and are formatted as they are written (see Figure 10-3). Some special tape marks are used to indicate the beginning or end of a data area (which may be composed of many data blocks). Information on tapes is always read and written in a sequential manner.

File Systems 87

| Interrecord Gap | Record Header | Data Record |

Figure 10-3   Typical Tape Format.

Files

A **file** is a named collection of data records on a secondary storage device. Files provide the means by which a task stores data for use at some later time. A data **record** within a file is simply a list of information elements which are accessed together, while a file name is attached to the file as a descriptor used to find and access the file at some future time. Systems usually place restrictions on file names and file sizes that are consistent with storage device and system hardware characteristics.

Generally, each secondary storage media **volume** (e.g., diskette, tape, disk pack) has a **directory** associated with it that lists the files existing on that volume. Each directory entry describes a particular file and may contain information such as:

1) File Name
2) Owner and/or Creator
3) Size
4) Volume Location (e.g., Track and Sector)
5) Attributes
6) Date/Time Created
7) Date/Time Last Used
8) Comments

In some multiuser systems, volume directories may contain more than file entries; some entries may describe other directories (normally one for each user). This type of hierarchical structure is very flexible and can be expanded to an unlimited number of directory levels. Hierarchical directories are useful in data base management systems where a variety of access mechanisms and protection levels are required. However, implementation of hierarchical directory structure usually requires considerable system overhead when files are accessed. Dedicated microprocessor and minicomputer systems often permit tasks to access disk storage devices directly via absolute sector read and write operations. To use this capability, disk storage areas must be predefined by the user or system programmer. This method of disk access is normally unprotected and a malfunctioning task could destroy data areas assigned to other tasks.

File Allocation

Files are allocated on disk devices by reserving a sufficient number of sectors to contain them. Some systems force these sectors to be contiguous on the media. This method leads to secondary storage fragmentation since, as files are created, updated, or deleted, free areas of the disk become separated from one another. Then, when a large file is created, these free areas cannot be used because they are not contiguous. In some cases, the file system may not be able to create a file even though there is sufficient free space on the disk. At this point **garbage collection** (also called **squeezing** or **compressing** the disk) must be performed.

A more flexible technique for file allocation is a linked list organization where the directory entry contains the location of the file's first sector, and each file sector contains the location of the next sector in the file. Rather than having a link to the next sector physically reside in each file sector, many systems create a set of pointer sectors for each file. Each of these sectors contains the locations for a fixed number of sectors within the file, and the number of pointer sectors needed for a file is determined from the file size by a simple ratio as demonstrated in Figure 10-4.

File Systems 89

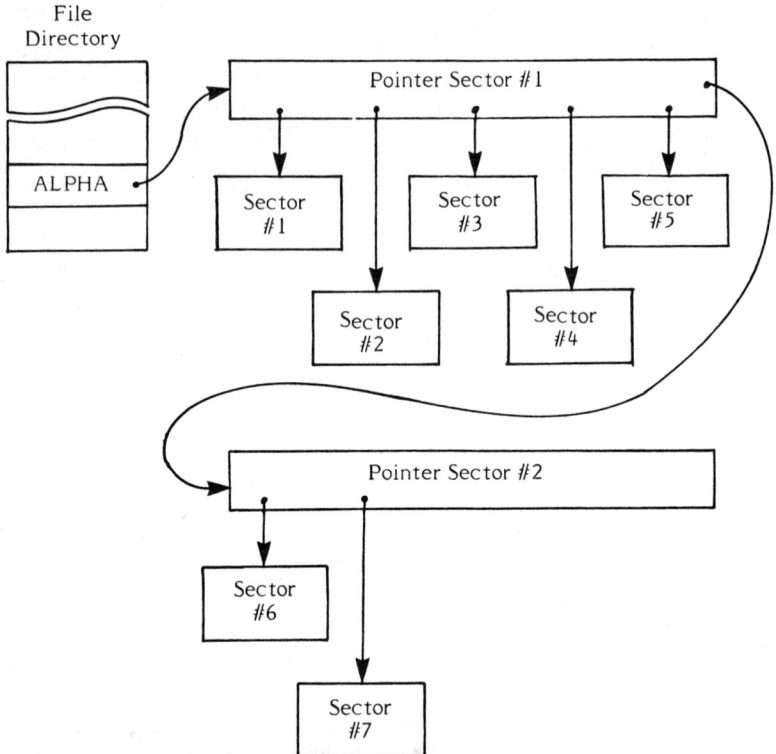

Figure 10-4 File Storage Utilizing Pointer Sectors. If each pointer sector contains n pointers, the number of pointer sectors required is m/n where m is the file size in sectors.

Allocation of file space in this manner presents much the same problems as the memory allocation discussed in Chapter 8; a free list of disk sectors must be maintained from which new file space is allocated and to which old file space is returned when a file is removed (deleted) from the system. A free list across the entire surface of the disk may cause excessive seeking and latency delays when file storage management is taking place. To avoid excessive delays, many systems use a free space allocation technique known as a **bit map**. A bit in the bit map is set aside for each sector on the media; a one indicates that the corresponding sector is allocated, a zero indicates that the corresponding sector is free. The first bit in the bit map corresponds to the first sector on the disk, and the last bit in the bit map corresponds to the last sector on the disk. The bit map is small in size since only one bit is used to represent a complete sector. The bit map is physically placed close to the directory so disk head movement is minimized. Allocation and freeing of sectors is accomplished by simply altering the bit map - no other sectors need be read, written or rewritten.

Access Methods

Two types of file access methods are used: **sequential access** and **random access**. Sequential access files must be processed a record at a time, in order. Card readers and line printers may be simulated as sequential access files. Files stored on magnetic tape are also sequential access files with the addition of a **backspace** capability to back up over one record at a time. Sequential files are useful where a sequence of data records are read, processed, and output in order; order entry, payroll, and billing files are used in this manner. Records within sequential access files may be of fixed or variable length.

On the other hand, any record in a random access file may be accessed by simply presenting its record number. It is easy to see how this is performed for files with a fixed record size, but a file with variable record sizes requires a special record **index table** as shown in Figure 10-5 where the location of each record is stored in order in this table.

Capabilities and Attributes

File access in most current systems is controlled by matching users and tasks with a set of permissible operations that they may perform on a given file. The term

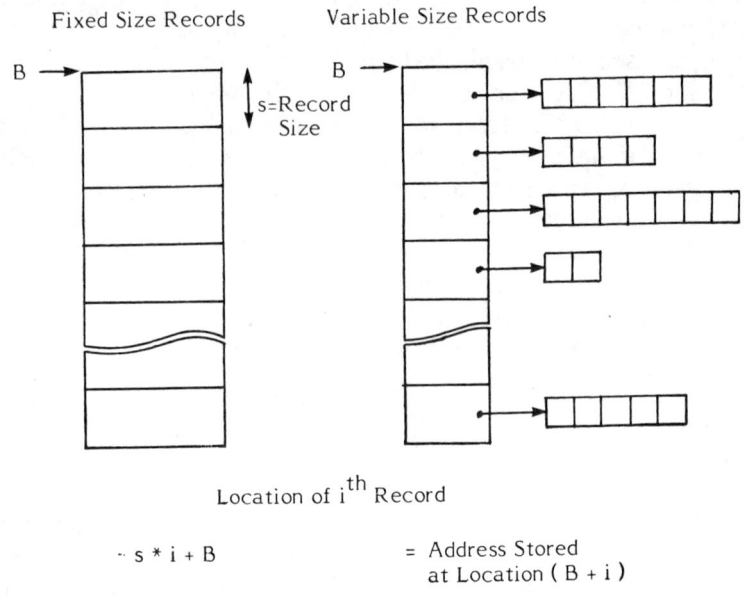

Figure 10-5 Fixed and Variable Size Records in Random Access Files.

capability is applied to the pairing of a user or task and the operations (commonly known as **attributes**) that may be performed. Users and tasks are generally classified as:

    1) Owner
    2) Project Associates or Partners
    3) Holders of a Special Keyword
    4) All Other Users

Each of these users may be granted file access with any combination of the following attributes:

    1) Invisible - user or task may not access directory information concerning the file.
    2) Read - user or task may read the file.
    3) Write - user or task may write the file.

4) Execute - user or task may execute the file.
5) Delete - user or task may delete the file.
6) Append/Update - user or task may add records to the file.
7) Change Attributes - user or task may change the file attributes.

More general resource security is discussed in detail in Chapter 11.

In some systems, files are also assigned a type attribute in order to check the validity of operations. Typical types are:

1) Object Code/Binary
2) Text
3) Library
4) Executable

File Services

The file system generally provides users and tasks with support services such as:

1) Create - Initialize a file by creating a directory entry and allocating disk space if required.

2) Delete - Destroy a file by removing the directory entry and freeing its disk space.

3) Rename - Change a file name in the directory.

4) Copy - Duplicate file data records in another file.

5) Concatenate - Join two or more files into a single file.

6) Open - Assign a file to a task for use.

File Systems

7) Close - Release a file (cancel the previous assignment) when a task has completed its use.

8) Attribute - Modify or set file attributes.

9) Assign/Connect - Connect a physical file to a logical I/O device.

10) Attach - Connect a file to a task as a logical segment in a virtual memory system (see Chapter 8).

Chapter II

System Security

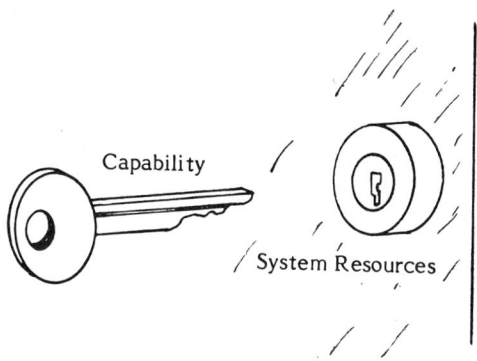

The topic of system security can be divided into four distinct areas:

1) Access Security - to permit only authorized personnel to gain access to the system.
2) Operating System Security - to guarantee integrity of operating system code and data structures.
3) Task Security - to protect task code and data structures in system memory from the errors of other tasks.
4) Resource Security - to preserve the integrity of the file system.

Access Security

Access to a computer system is controlled by a variety of methods, many of which are procedural and not associated with the operating system software. For instance, the system may be placed in a restricted location such as the control room of a plant or in a university computing center. In this manner, a certain level of security is implemented mechanically by denying admission to unauthorized personnel. In some cases admission is controlled by magnetic card/badge readers that are connected to the computer system.

Once a user or programmer has gained physical access to the system, several levels of software restrictions may be provided. The first and most general level of system access is the ability to **LOG ON** to the system. In this manner, a user identifies himself to the system and causes it to perform any required functions. In order to prevent unauthorized personnel from logging into the system as authorized users, systems often require a password before a user is granted access. This password is initially entered into the system by the operations manager when a new user is first entered into the system access lists. After successfully logging on to the system, a user may normally change his password at any time. Some system functions and/or status information are available only to users with special authorization. These functions may be controlled by additional passwords. For example, the operations manager requires access to restricted system data structures in order to install new users into the system. This access is controlled either by requiring an additional password or by automatically granting special privileges when a user logs onto the system.

Operating System Security

Operating system security deals with the ability of the operating system to withstand accidental or deliberate damage. This means that system code and data structures must be protected against modification by unauthorized tasks. Additionally, I/O devices that are controlled by the system must also be protected. Some computer architectures include instructions that can only be executed in a special **privileged mode**. In use, no user task is permitted to enter the privileged mode and therefore only the operating system can execute instructions that affect system security. In some cases, the operating system code and data structures are contained in a specific memory area that can only be accessed by instructions in the privileged mode. Operating system security is the most important aspect of total system security since violations of system data integrity quickly cause the system to cease functioning.

Task Security

Task security revolves around the issue of a task's vulnerability to the errors and malfunctions of other tasks. Generally, total task security involves either hardware memory protection or slower execution while each instruction is simulated and checked for memory protection violations. If a task's memory image (including all context information) is protected, it will correctly execute when

System Security

restarted even if other tasks have suffered catastrophic failures. Typically hardware memory protection is provided by **length registers** or **limit registers** used in conjunction with each segment's base register. The base register contains the lowest valid segment address and the limit register contains the highest valid segment address. If a length register is used, the sum of its contents and the contents of the base address register defines the highest valid segment address. If a task attempts to reference data outside of a segment, a memory **protection violation** is recorded, task execution is suspended, and the appropriate operating system functions are invoked.

Resource Security

Even if its code is preserved, a task cannot perform its function if the data it acts on has been destroyed. When the data is contained in system memory, general task security techniques such as memory protection are sufficient. However, if task data is contained on secondary storage, this must also be protected against damage. Resource security in most common systems is enforced by the file system as discussed in Chapter 10.

Recently, however, resource security has been viewed in a new light which encompasses memory, data, and task security. Most current security techniques are subsets of more general methods constructed from the concepts of **classes, monitors,** and **capabilities.**

A class is a data structure such as a task segment, file, stack, or I/O device and a set of valid access operations that may be performed on the structure. For example:

    1) task segment - valid operations are *READ, WRITE, EXECUTE*
    2) file - valid operations are *READ, WRITE, EXECUTE, APPEND, RENAME*
    3) stack - valid operations are *PUSH, POP, EXCHANGE, DUPLICATE*

4) I/O device - valid operations are *READ, WRITE, STATUS, CONTROL*

A monitor is a class organized in such a way that no two tasks may use the access operations at the same time. A monitor is a structured way of implementing synchronization rules (Chapter 6) and preserving data integrity since a task that wishes to access a data structure must wait until any current access has been completed.

Capabilities

Unauthorized use of the valid operations on a class may be prohibited by one of two methods. The first involves tables or lists that are maintained by the operating system. These lists detail, for each class, the tasks and users that are permitted to access the class and the operations they may perform. In order to make these tables manageable, most operating systems divide the user/task community into four groups:

1) Owner - Creator of a file or user/task assigned to manage a device. For instance, in most large systems, a special user, designated as *SYSTEM* owns line printers and tape drives.

2) Partner - A project associate usually known to the operating system because his identification tables contain the same project number.

3) Keyholders - Users/tasks sometimes require limited access to files on an exception or limited time interval basis (e.g., for a month). In this case, a special key is attached to the file and anyone who presents the key for an access may utilize the file.

4) All Other Users - Any user or task which does not fall into one or more of the above categories.

System Security

Each of these user groups may then access resources according to the attributes contained in the system tables. For instance, a language translator may only be executed by most users, while it may be read or executed by all system programmers, and it may be read, written, or executed by the developer.

The second protection method utilizes a data structure known as a **capability**. Each capability pairs a resource (e.g., task segment, line printer, or file) with the set of operations that may be performed on the resource by the task. All tasks have associated capability lists that must contain a capability for each resource which the task intends to access. Capability lists are usually contained within special **capability segments**. The ability to create or modify capability segments is itself a capability which is reserved for only selected system tasks. It is interesting to note that the privileged mode in many systems may be implemented by capabilities, where privileged instructions form a resource class with the *EXECUTE* operation defined. The capability to *EXECUTE* these instructions is granted only to system tasks.

Two implementation problem areas exist with respect to the use of general capability structures in a computer system. The first has to do with the way in which a capability is passed to subtasks or cooperating tasks. If physical copies of capabilities are passed throughout the system, the destruction of a capability implies that all its copies must be reclaimed. This can be a time consuming action, searching through all capabilities within the system. If instead, no copies are made, but pointers to the original capability are passed among tasks, each capability access could incur large processing overhead as chains of indirect references are followed up.

The second area deals with the ability for a task to receive and transmit capabilities for support operations that it is not permitted to utilize directly. This would be the case, for example, when a task wishes to perform I/O to a terminal. The task must pass the terminal access capability to an I/O driver, but the task should not be permitted to use that capability to directly control I/O to the terminal. Neither of these problems is trivial, and research is still being done on efficient capability implementations.

Archival Storage

In addition to resource security, the topic of file system security must deal with archival and back-up storage in order to recover information after system failures. Most systems provide the following forms of archival or back-up storage:

1) File System Dump - All files in the secondary storage directory are written onto a large backing store such as magnetic tape.

2) Incremental Dump - All files in the secondary storage directory modified or created after a given date are written onto the backing store.

3) File Save - An individual file or group of files (e.g., all files belonging to a given user) from secondary storage is written onto the backing store.

4) File Restore - An individual file or group of files is read from the backing store and written to a secondary storage device.

Appendix A

Glossary of Operating System Terms

Abstract Machine - A formal definition of a processor (instruction set and memory access specification). Abstract machines are often considerably different from available hardware and are simulated on conventional computers by special programs. Interpreters translate source text into abstract machine instructions.

Accept - A system service used for task communication and synchronization that extracts a message from the appropriate mailbox, but does not suspend the requesting task if the mailbox is empty. This permits tasks to check multiple mailboxes periodically for messages.

Access Time - The amount of time required to fetch a given data element. This time may be as short as 25 nanoseconds for data in a cache memory buffer or as long as hundreds of milliseconds for a flexible diskette sector access.

Accounting - Information that an operating system may retain about each job in order to produce reports on system usage and billing. This information usually includes job/user name, account number, date and time, run time, I/O channel usage, etc.

Activate - Another term for the Start system service.

Allocate - A system service used by a task to request memory for message or I/O buffers.

Assembler - A language translator that translates text input into machine code (to be executed directly on a processor). The input language is very close to the actual machine instruction set and one text line usually translates into a single instruction.

Assign - An operating system function which sets aside a resource such as a printer, tape drive, or terminal for use by the requesting task. Normally a resource can only be assigned to a single task at a given time. However, in some cases, as with disk files, multiple tasks may concurrently be assigned the resource for *read only* access.

Associative Memory - Another term for Content-Addressable Memory.

Attach - A system service of the I/O subsystem that connects a physical device to a logical device. Thus tasks may be written to be independent of the physical devices and the user or another task may attach any legal device when the task executes.

Attributes - The set of operations that may be performed on a resource.

Backspace - An operation whose function is to move backwards in a sequential file one record at a time.

Base Register - A high speed storage location that contains the address of the first data word or instruction of a segment. All addresses within the segment are referenced to the start of the segment, and during execution, the physical address of each memory reference is calculated by simply adding the contents of the base register to the relative addresses contained within the segment. Thus, relocation is easily accomplished by simply moving a segment in memory and placing the new address in the base register.

Batch - A type of operating system where jobs are processed one at a time and a job must complete its execution before the next is begun.

Best Fit - An algorithm for memory allocation that searches the memory free list for the unused memory block that is closest in size to that needed by the requesting task.

Bit Map - A data structure utilized by some file systems to assist with file space allocation. A bit in the bit map is set aside for each sector on the media - a one indicates that the corresponding sector is allocated, and a zero indicates that the corresponding sector is free. The bit map is placed physically close to the directory so disk head movement is minimized.

Blocked - Another term for the Suspended task state.

Breakpoint - The address at which task execution is to be suspended. Many systems feature the capability to suspend task execution before or after a breakpoint address is executed, when a read or write to a breakpoint address is attempted, or when an I/O operation to a breakpoint address is executed.

Buffer - A temporary storage area, usually used for message and I/O transfers.

Buffer Memory - A high speed local memory area that is used by I/O processors to store transmitted and/or received data. Normally, buffer memories are used either because a peripheral device has higher speed requirements than general system memory can support or because additional processing must be performed on the data by the I/O processor either before or after transmission.

Busy Wait - A situation in which a task waits for access to a resource by continuously testing a flag. Thus, even though the task is not performing any useful work during its wait, the processor that it runs on is busy executing test instructions, and no other task can execute on that processor.

Cache - A small but very high speed memory buffer situated between the processor and main memory in a computer system. It operates on the principle that certain memory locations tend to be accessed very often (normally for reads). Thus, when a main memory location is read, it is stored in the cache at the same time. Any further read references to this location are automatically routed to the cache. A write access usually writes to both main memory and the cache. Since a cache represents many non-contiguous main memory locations, content addressable registers are usually used to determine when a main memory location is currently stored in the cache. One problem that arises with a cache has to do with the handling of I/O channels that can write into main memory without the processor's knowledge. In order for the cache to be correct at all times, it usually has to monitor all write accesses to main memory.

When a main memory location is read (that is not currently in the cache), some large cache buffers automatically read 8, 16, or more locations into the cache. The reasoning for this action is that programs tend to access data locally (plus or minus one location) and this new data will already be in the cache by the time it is needed.

Capability - A data structure utilized to enforce system security. Each capability pairs a resource with the operations that may be performed on it by a given task. Thus, a task may not access a resource unless it carries the proper capability.

Capability Segment - A segment that contains capabilities and may only be modified by a few system services within the operating system.

Catalog - Another name for a Directory.

Chaining - A technique of linking physically separated instructions or operations (to be executed by a processor) into a list. Once started, the processor continues to perform operations and link to the next instruction until the end of the list is found. This method of operation is used extensively with I/O processors so that complex data transfers may be accomplished with minimal task intervention.

Channel - Another term for an I/O Channel.

Checksum - An error detection technique that is easily implemented in software. It is often used to check code/data in ROM/RAM where single bit errors are most likely.

Class - A data structure and the operations defined on that structure.

Close - A system service used with disk files and other shared resources. This service informs the operating system that a task has completed use of a resource.

Communication - The facility whereby one task can pass data and commands to another. For example, an application task may pass an output buffer to a printer control task. In some operating systems this communication facility is generalized to permit tasks to reside in separate physical locations and transmit data across a communication link such as a standard telephone line, leased line, or microwave link.

Compiler - A language translator that translates the text of a high level language (e.g., FORTRAN or COBOL) into machine code. Compilers automatically assign, save, and restore registers and generate subroutine linkages. Thus, a programmer does not need to worry about system housekeeping and can concentrate on the application.

Compress - Another term for Garbage Collection.

Concurrent Processes - Processes or tasks whose execution overlaps in time. They may be cooperating/ interacting (communicating with one another) or independent.

Consumable Resource - A resource such as an I/O buffer or message that is produced (e.g., filled) by one task and consumed (e.g., read and acted on) and freed by another task.

Consumer - A task that uses a resource. For example, the printer device driver is a consumer of output line buffers produced by the assembler.

Content-Addressable Memory - A memory that is addressable by its contents rather than by location. For instance, instead of reading the data at location $1A3_{16}$, data is read from the location that contains "BETA". Content-addressable memories are often used in segmented systems to contain recently-used segment base addresses. Segment names and base addresses are paired in memory locations. To access the segment "ALPHA", all memory locations are simultaneously searched for "ALPHA". This typically occurs within 25 to 100 nanoseconds. If "ALPHA" is found, the next data value can be loaded into a base register for a segment access. When content-addressable memories are not used in a segmented system, the segment name table must be accessed for each segment reference. This requires additional slow main memory cycles.

Contention - A situation that occurs when more than one task vies for a single resource.

Context - That body of changeable information that belongs to a task or process and must be saved when a task's execution is suspended so that it can later be restarted without error. This information typically includes the contents of the processor registers, the program counter, I/O and interrupt status, and data memory.

Copy - A system support task that copies data blocks from one storage device/location to another.

CRC - An abbreviation for Cyclic Redundancy Code, an error checking technique that provides a high degree of error detection. It is often used for data transmission links and disk controllers where burst errors are frequent.

Glossary

Create - A system service that initializes a structure by entering information such as its name, size, etc., into system tables. At this point the operating system knows the structure exists, hence the term creation. Other functions may also be performed depending on the type of structure to be created. For instance, creation of a file may mean default allocation of a prespecified number of disk blocks.

Critical Region - Another term for a Critical Section.

Critical Section - A portion of software that accesses a shared resource and must be protected so that while one task is performing the access (executing the software), no other task is permitted to access the same resource. For example, when updating a 32 bit floating point number, all four bytes must be written before another task may read the data. In some cases, interrupts must be disabled when this code is executed if a higher priority task may require access to the same resource.

Cycle Stealing - A memory access technique where an I/O processor is synchronized to the general processor's memory cycles in such a way that it *steals* memory cycles between those of the general processor. This is possible on systems where the memory cycle time is significantly shorter than the processor execution cycle.

Data Base - A large and complete collection of information that covers a variety of subject areas. For instance, a company's payroll data base contains employee number, social security number, classification, age, wage rate, salary history, etc., about each employee. A medical diagnostic data base might contain symptoms for all common diseases or injuries.

Data Structure - A mechanism, including both storage layout and access rules, by which information may be stored and retrieved within a computer system. Data structures may reside in memory or on secondary storage. System tables such as task descriptors and symbol tables, matrices of numerical data, and data files are common examples of data structures.

Date - A system service that supplies the current date to requesting tasks.

Deadlock - A situation that occurs when all tasks within a system are suspended waiting for resources that have already been assigned to other tasks that are also waiting for additional resources. Thus, the system can perform no useful work unless tasks are destroyed and their resources reclaimed.

Deadly Embrace - Another term for a Deadlock.

Debugger - A system software utility that aids a programmer in removing errors from his software.

Delete - This system service is the same as Destroy. However, in some cases the structure may not actually be destroyed, but just removed from the system tables.

Demand Paging - A paging algorithm in a virtual storage system where pages are not loaded into physical memory until a reference is made to that page.

Destroy - A system service that removes structure information from system tables. At this point, the structure ceases to exist from the operating system point of view, hence the term destruction. Depending on the type of structure, other functions may also be performed. For example, destruction of a file usually results in freeing of storage space that may then be used for other files.

Device - A unit of peripheral hardware, usually for Input and/or Output such as a printer, terminal, or card reader.

Device Driver - Another term for a Driver.

Diagnostics - System support tasks (usually supplied with an operating system) that test memory, interrupts, timers, and peripheral devices.

Direct I/O - A facility, usually specified as part of the computer system architecture whereby input from or output to peripheral devices is performed under direct processor control via special I/O instructions. For example, *OUTPUT the ACCUMULATOR to PORT X* is a direct I/O instruction. Most microprocessors support only direct I/O.

Directory - A data structure containing entries for each file in the file system. Each directory entry contains information about the file name, owner, access rights, size, etc. Directory entries on some systems may be pointers to other subdirectories.

Dispatcher - Another term for a Scheduler.

Distributed Processing - A multiprocessing technique where each processor has a specific task or set of tasks to perform. These processors transfer commands and data via a standard communication interface, often SDLC or IEEE-488. In some cases, programs are transferred between processing units. However, this capability is normally utilized for power-on loads or control algorithm changes rather than general load sharing.

DMA - An I/O processor memory access technique whereby the system processor is placed in a wait mode (usually called HOLD in microprocessor systems) while the I/O processor transfers data to or from memory at the maximum memory data rate. When the I/O transfer is complete, the processor resumes executing.

Driver - A system software module that directly controls the data transfer to and from I/O peripherals. Some operating systems also include the capability to add custom device drivers for hardware that is unique to a given system or installation.

Dual Port Memory - A memory subsystem design that provides two complete paths (address, data, control) and therefore two processors (usually a general processor and an I/O processor) may request memory cycles asynchronously. Since the memory can only perform one function at a time, dual port arbitration logic is designed to permit accesses on a first-come, first-served basis, with one path (or port) having priority for simultaneous requests. In practice, dual port memory design provides significantly higher throughput because memory cycles are considerably shorter than processor cycles.

Dynamic Priority - A form of scheduling in that a task's execution priority varies depending on the system environment. For example, it is common for time sharing systems to initially give large tasks low priority, but raise the priority periodically as the task waits to execute. This assures that low priority tasks will not be locked out of execution time by small, high priority tasks.

Editor - A system utility that permits a programmer to create, edit, concatenate, and delete complete files and portions of files on secondary storage media. Editors operate almost exclusively on text files. Two types of editors are common: character editors and line editors. Line editors treat a text file on a line by line basis, while character editors treat a text file as a series of characters, and line delimiters (carriage return, line feed) are treated like any other characters.

Entry Point - The programmer defined instruction at which a task is to begin execution.

Error Code - An error detection technique where a bit pattern (usually a byte or word) is computed from a block of data. This pattern may be recomputed at a later time (e.g., after data transmission) to determine whether the data has been changed. Some codes not only detect errors but contain all information necessary to correct them. These codes are used to provide error correcting memory.

Error Correcting Memory - A memory design where an error code is stored in conjunction with the actual data byte or word so that single bit errors may be corrected and multiple bit errors may be detected.

Error Logging - An operating system service that keeps track of device or task malfunctions for post-mortem review. This service usually consists of a short module to gather information at each error occurrence, and a longer user-initiated module to format and print error information at a later time.

Event - A condition used to synchronize task execution. An event may be a timer or I/O interrupt, the arrival of a message at a task's mailbox, or the occurrence of an exception condition.

Event Flag - An easily implemented synchronization mechanism that can be used for passing messages and data buffers between two cooperating tasks.

Exception - A condition which is out of the ordinary in normal task execution, e.g., arithmetic overflow.

Executive - Another term for an Operating System.

Exchange - Another term for a Mailbox.

FIFO - An abbreviation for First-In First-Out.

File - A collection of data, normally stored on a secondary storage device such as magnetic tape or disk. Files are usually named, have an owner, and may be protected against erroneous or malicious damage by the file system.

File System - System software modules that manage files on secondary storage media. This software usually provides functions to create, delete, or rename files, permit reading and writing of existing files, and enforce system protection strategies.

First Fit - An algorithm for memory allocation that searches the free list only long enough to find an unused memory block that is large enough to satisfy the requesting task.

First-In First-Out - A data access mechanism that implements a queue. Data elements are always extracted from the data structure in the same order that they are entered (the first element in is the first element out).

Foreground/Background - A type of operating system with a combination of real time and either batch or multitasking capabilities. This type of system is used to permit time critical programs to operate in the *foreground* and execute with high priority while *background* assemblies, edits, etc., are also going on at much lower priority. Foreground programs always have priority over background work. This type of operating system usually has the capability to protect the foreground from the background, and is used in applications such as process control.

Format - A system utility that initializes secondary storage media with information necessary to assure that data can subsequently be read or written without error. The information is usually closely related to the read/write hardware. An example of a popular formatting technique is the IBM soft-sectored format for single density diskettes.

Fragmentation - The division of a contiguous storage area such as main memory or secondary storage in a way that causes areas to be wasted. For instance, in most paged systems, whole pages are always allocated, even when a program or data segment is smaller than the page size. In segmented systems or in a system with dynamic memory allocation, continually loading and swapping new tasks will almost always cause small areas of memory to become unusable. At the point where this wasted space impacts system performance, most operating systems perform garbage collection.

Free - A system service that returns allocated memory blocks to the memory manager for reuse.

Free List - A list of memory locations that are currently unused and may be allocated by the memory manager to requesting tasks. Free lists are usually organized as linked lists of memory blocks, where each block contains the size of the block and a pointer to the next block in the list.

Friendly Environment - A software environment in which all software is adequately tested and therefore one task will not interfere with or cause errors in the execution of another task.

Garbage Collection - A system function contained in most operating systems whose memory (main or secondary) is subject to fragmentation. This function reallocates the affected memory in such a way as to reclaim all wasted space. This is usually a drastic and time consuming step, and is only invoked on operator command or when memory utilization is very low and seriously affecting system efficiency. This function is sometimes known as Squeezing, Compressing, or Compacting.

Handler - Another term for a Driver.

Hard Error - An error in magnetic media, electromechanical devices or electronics which is repeatable.

Hierarchical Directory - A means of organizing secondary storage file diectories where directory entries may describe either files or other directories. Some multiuser systems have a master disk directory with one subdirectory for each user.

High Level Language - A sophisticated yet easy to use language (written words and special punctuation) that allows a programmer to write software without being concerned with housekeeping functions (e.g., register allocation) or optimization. Common high level languages are FORTRAN, BASIC, COBOL, ALGOL, APL, PL/1, PL/M, and PASCAL.

Hostile Environment - A system software environment in which it is assumed that both hardware and software may fail in any way, and the system is required either to continue running or shut itself down in an orderly manner.

In Circuit Emulation (ICE) - A capability provided on many microcomputer development systems that enables a system designer to use the facilities of the development system to debug prototype hardware and software. Physically, this is accomplished via an umbilical cable from the development system that plugs into the microprocessor socket in the prototype system.

Index Table - A table utilized for reading and writing random access files with variable record sizes. A file index table contains an entry for each record of the file, detailing the size and location of the record.

Indirect I/O - A facility, usually specified as part of the computer system architecture, whereby input from or output to peripheral devices is performed by a unit separate from the main processor. This unit is commonly called a Channel or I/O Processor.

Install - A system utility that copies a newly generated operating system in place of an old version.

Instruction Pointer - A register within the processing element of a computer that contains the address of the next instruction to be executed. It is automatically incremented by the processor and modified by conditional and unconditional transfer instructions.

Interactive Debugger - A system software utility that permits a user to examine his task while it executes by stopping it at given points (usually called breakpoints) and displaying and changing memory/register contents.

Interleaving - A track formatting technique utilized with moving and fixed head disk media in which sectors are not stored sequentially. Using this technique, multiple sectors may be read or written sequentially with a minimum of disk latency. This is made possible by placing sectors on a track in such a way that the time required to process a single sector is slightly less than the time required for the disk to rotate to the start of the next logical sector.

Interleave Factor - The number of sectors between a given sector and the next logical sector on a disk track when implementing an interleaving strategy.

Interpreter - A language translator that accepts high level language (e.g., BASIC or PASCAL) input text and translates this text into a special intermediate code that is simulated (interpreted) by a system program. Usually this intermediate code cannot be directly executed on a general purpose processor.

Interrupt - A signal from an external source such as a timer or I/O device that causes a processor to interrupt execution of the current task. Most operating systems use this occurrence to reschedule tasks for execution and therefore dedicate a timer interrupt for this purpose.

Interval Timer - A hardware or software clock which generates an interrupt after a specified period of time has elapsed.

I/O Channel - An I/O processing unit that controls all input from and output to peripheral devices in some computer systems. Often a channel has its own instruction set dedicated to I/O type operations, and after setup via operating system software, a program need only execute a *START I/O* instruction to perform complete I/O transactions. In most system architectures, channel processors operate in parallel (concurrently) with the general task processor, thus significantly increasing system throughput.

I/O Executive - Another term for an I/O Subsystem.

I/O Mapped - A method of implementing system input and output that provides special *INPUT* and *OUTPUT* instruction by which I/O ports are accessed. I/O mapping requires separate hardware address decoding for memory and I/O transfers.

I/O Processor - Another term for an I/O Channel.

I/O Subsystem - A set of system software modules that control all Input and Output within a system. An I/O subsystem normally contains device drivers, performs buffer administration, handles error conditions, and provides a uniform interfacing structure by which tasks may request I/O transfers.

I/O Supervisor - Another term for an I/O Subsystem.

ISAM - An abbreviation for Indexed Sequential Access Method. This technique for finding records within a file assigns a number or key to each record and creates a separate file index. To access a record, the record number or key is looked up in the index to find the actual record location within the file. This organization is useful for sorting files according to more than one record item, for example when a payroll file must be sorted by both employee number and social security number. By creating more than one file index and sorting each index according to the required item, the same physical file may appear to be multiple files.

JCL - An abbreviation for Job Control Language.

Job - A collection of tasks, grouped and run together in order to perform a specific function.

Job Control Language - A special computer command language designed for use in batch systems to inform the systems software and computer operator of unique requirements for the running of a computer program.

Kernel - The most basic portion of an operating system, usually supporting only task synchronization, scheduling, communication, and the most rudimentary of memory allocation capabilities.

Language Translator - A system program that translates text written in one language to another language. Assemblers, interpreters, and compilers are examples of language translators.

Length Register - A high speed memory location used in conjunction with a base register in task security implementations. The base register contains the lowest physical address of the segment and the contents of the base register plus the contents of the limit register is the highest physical address of the segment.

Librarian - A system program that is responsible for creating, editing, and deleting software libraries.

Library - A collection of system and/or user tasks which may be executed by other tasks in the system. The major reason for libraries is to prevent software redesign each time a function is needed by a task. For example, an I/O driver would reside in the system library and be accessed by user tasks for I/O service.

Linked List - A data structure in which each element contains a pointer to its predecessor or successor (singly linked list) or both (doubly linked list).

Linker - A system software module that connects previously assembled/compiled tasks into a unit that can be loaded into memory and executed.

Loader - A system software module that moves user tasks from secondary storage into memory for execution. It may also perform relocation computations as required.

Load Module - A software module that is ready to be loaded into memory and executed. A load module has all static relocation and linkage operations completed.

Load Sharing - A scheduling technique in multiprocessing systems whereby a task is executed by the next available processor. In order to make this technique operate successfully, all processors must be identical and have identical memory addressing capabilities.

Logical Address - A means of addressing data and/or program instructions in such a way as to be independent of the physical memory structure of a given machine. For example, a logical address may be specified as: WORD 5 OF SEGMENT ALPHA. Of course, when the program is run, this logical address is translated by either hardware of software on the target machine into a physical address within the machine structure.

Logical Device - A reference to an I/O device by name or number without regard to the exact nature of the I/O device. At execution time, the operator, or another task assigns a physical device to the logical device name or number. The I/O subsystem then assures that the proper device drivers are utilized to perform the I/O transfers.

Log On - A mechanism by which a computer system user identifies himself and gains access to system facilities.

Mailbox - A system data structure that handles task communication. Tasks send messages to and receive messages from Mailboxes.

Memory Dump - A system utility used in software debugging that prints the contents of all or a portion of main memory on the printer.

Memory Manager - A system software module that manages the physical memory resource and controls memory allocation for tasks in the system. In a virtual memory or paging system, this module also translates logical addresses into physical addresses and implements the page fetch, placement, and replacement algorithms.

Memory Mapped - A method of implementing system input and output that provides I/O ports that are accessed as if they were memory locations. However, the term memory mapping does not imply that all memory operations (e.g., increment memory) may be performed on a memory mapped I/O port. This is due to the fact that some peripheral control registers may be either *read only* or *write only*. In fact, some designs mate write only control data with read only status data in order to save memory adddresses. Thus, writes and reads of the same memory location may have no connection to one another.

Message - A unit of communication between tasks. In a typical system, a message usually contains a header with information about message size, the sending task, etc.

Microcomputer Development System - A system designed exclusively to aid in the development of microprocessor systems. Microcomputer development systems enable a designer to develop software and hardware as if many standard operating system utilities were present in his final design. However, these utilities actually reside in the development system and therefore do not require costly additions to every shipped system.

Module - A section of software that has well defined inputs and outputs and may be tested independently of other software.

Monitor - The term monitor has two meanings when applied to operating system functions: a) In the microprocessor sense, it typically refers to a small system software executive that permits operator interaction with the microprocessor system for the purpose of examining and changing the contents of registers and memory locations, performing I/O to the console and printer, and performing simple debugging of user programs, while b) in the software engineering sense, it refers to a common data structure and the set of operations defined on that structure such that no two tasks can use the operations at the same time, thus implementing a task synchronization rule. A task that wishes to access the data structure must wait until any current access has been completed.

Multiprocessing - The ability of an operating system to support multiple processors. Generally, in order to make the operating system task manageable, all processors are equivalent and interchangeable, although this is not a requirement.

Multiprogramming - Another term for Multitasking.

Glossary

Multitasking - The ability of an operating system to permit multiple tasks to run concurrently.

Multiterminal - The ability of an operating system task to support multiple terminals. Note that this capability does not imply Multiuser capability since on some systems, multiple terminals must be under control of the same task or cooperating tasks, and all users are therefore forced to use the same software. For example, order entry processing is an example of one task (order entry) and many terminals.

Multiuser - The ability of an operating system to support more than one independent user. Sometimes multi-terminal systems are billed as multiuser systems, but a true multiuser system should allow users to independently use system resources.

Mutual Exclusion - A process synchronization rule which prohibits more than one task from using the same resource at the same time.

Non-Preemptive Scheduling - A scheduling algorithm where a task does not stop executing until it is complete. Non-preemptive scheduling techniques attempt to pick the tasks for execution which keep average turn-around time to a minimum. However, once a long task begins execution, all other tasks must wait until it completes regardless of relative priorities.

Nucleus - Another term for a Kernel.

Object Code - The output of an assembler or compiler that will execute on the target processor. Note that linking and loading may be required before this code can execute directly on the processor.

Open - A system service used with disk files and other shared resources. This service informs the operating system of the manner in which a task intends to use a given resource.

Operating System - A collection of system software that permits user written tasks to interface to the machine hardware and interact with other tasks in a straightforward, efficient, and safe manner.

Overhead - The amount of processing time required by the operating system to perform housekeeping tasks such as paging, swapping, and scheduling. This time is usually expressed as a percentage of total available time. If system overhead is quoted as 20%, then user programs can only utilize 48 seconds (80%) of each minute of processor execution time.

Overlay - A technique used to execute programs which are larger than the available memory size in systems without paging or segmentation capabilities. To utilize this method, a program must be manually divided into a number of mutually exclusive groups of software modules. Any software common to more than one overlay is included in the *root* overlay. The root must remain in system memory at all times and other overlays are loaded and executed one at a time in a designated memory area. This loading is normally performed by the operating system at the request of the root overlay.

P - A primitive and indivisible operation that tests the status of a semaphore "gate". If the gate is open, this operation immediately closes and locks it, permitting the requesting task to enter a critical section and access shared data. If the gate is closed, the requesting task must wait until it is reopened.

Page - An artificial division of memory in order to facilitate memory management in multiprogramming systems. Pages are normally fixed size memory blocks between 512 bytes and 4096 bytes in length.

Page Fault - A condition that occurs when the logical address referenced by a task is not currently available in physical memory. At this point, a special algorithm is executed that finds the page containing the referenced address, determines where to locate it in physical memory, swaps out any page required to get the new page into memory, loads the page into memory, and finally returns control to the faulted task.

Performance Monitoring - System support software and/or hardware used to measure the performance of a computer system by timing and recording the execution of various tasks and modules. This timing information is then used by system analysts to tune the system for maximum efficiency by changing system tables and parameters or rewriting tasks to improve throughput.

Physical Address - The address of an existing system memory location.

Physical Device - An actual peripheral hardware device such as a line printer, terminal, card reader, or paper tape punch which is attached to a computer system.

Pool - An area of memory managed by the memory manager and reserved for allocation to requesting tasks. All allocated memory is returned to the pool after use. It may then be reallocated to other tasks. Memory for consumable resources such as messages or I/O buffers is often allocated from predefined pools.

Position Independent Code - Executable code which runs independent of the physical memory location at which it is loaded. This usually implies that the code contains only relative transfer instructions, or that all addressing is done via base registers.

Preemptive Scheduling - A means of scheduling where a high priority task will preempt execution of a lower priority task as soon as the high priority task is ready to run, usually after an interrupt.

Priority Scheduling - A scheduling algorithm where each task is given a priority, and the next task to execute is the one in the Ready List with the highest priority. Priorities may be static or dynamic. With static priorities, it is possible that some low priority tasks will never run due to the frequency and execution duration of higher priority tasks. This is very unhealthy in a Time Sharing System environment where it is necessary to guarantee that all tasks will receive some processor time on a regular basis. For these systems, the task priority is often changed as a function of time, so that the longer a task waits to execute, the higher its priority becomes.

Privileged - Instructions that may only be executed by system software. Set Interrupt Mask, Load Base Register, Load Protection Register, and Start I/O are examples of privileged operations. Some computer systems execute in one of two operational modes: normal and privileged. System software executes in the privileged mode and may execute all processor instructions. User tasks operate in the normal mode and the system is protected against many task malfunctions.

Process - Another term for a task.

Processor - A device that can execute the instructions of a task. It can execute one task at a time.

Producer - A task that generates a resource to be used by another task. For example, the assembler task is a producer of output line buffers to be consumed by the printer device driver.

Protection - An operating system service that prevents a task from interfering with the execution of another task.

Protection Violation - An attempt by a task to access a protected resource, or perform an unauthorized operation on an assigned resource. For example, attempting to write a *read only* file, or attempting to execute a privileged instruction will generate a protection violation.

Pure Code - Another term for Reentrant Code.

Queue - A data structure in which the first element in is the first element out; this data structure works in the same manner as a supermarket checkout line.

Random Access File - A type of file structure in which data may be accessed in a random manner, irregardless of its position within the file.

Ready - A task state in which a given task is prepared to execute.

Ready List - A system list of tasks that are in the Ready task state, meaning that they are ready to be executed on a processor.

Real Time - A type of operating system that supports on-line equipment having critical time constraints. Events must be handled promptly (within set timing limits). Most process control and military command/control systems are real time systems.

Real Time Clock - A system clock that indicates actual elapsed time from some reference time (e.g., midnight).

Record - A set of data elements that are logically accessed together. On a secondary storage medium, this can also be used to indicate the smallest set of data elements that are stored contiguously on the medium.

Reentrant Code - Code that may be executed simultaneously by more than one task. Thus, the code cannot be self-modifying, and each task must maintain its own data area. This does not imply that tasks will actually execute the code simultaneously, although this could occur in a multiprocessor system.

Register - A high speed memory location associated with a processor. Registers are normally used to store intermediate data and addresses within a program in order to speed overall execution time. Due to the high speed requirements and cost, the number of registers within a processor is usually limited to 8 or 16 storage locations, although some processors have a few hundred.

Release - A system service that informs the operating system that a task no longer requires use of a resource.

Relocation - The process of moving the location of a program in system memory. Relocation may either be static or dynamic. Static relocation means that all program addresses are assigned and fixed before the program is loaded into memory. Dynamic relocation refers to a technique that requires all program addresses to be relative to some base address and programs may be relocated at any time by moving the program code and changing the base address.

Rename - The act of changing the name of a data structure. This function is commonly supplied as a system service of the file system in order to change file names.

Resource - Assets of a computer system that the operating system can use and/or allocate to tasks for their use. Assets such as memory, disk storage space, printers and terminals as well as processors in multiprocessing systems, are typical system resources.

Resource Allocation - The operating system function of assigning resources to tasks that request them. Resources such as peripherals (printers, terminals, and card readers) and main memory are allocated to tasks based on their availability. Note that resource allocation can be a very difficult problem since deadlocks can easily occur where one task can't run until it gets another resource and the task holding that resource can't run until the previous task gives up one of its resources.

Response Time - The elapsed time from the entry of a command until its execution is complete. This term is usually used to represent the time it takes for a Time Sharing System to respond to a user command line.

Restore - A system utility that reloads a file to secondary storage from an archive volume such as magnetic or paper tape.

Retry - An attempt to provide automatic error recovery (usually for I/O operations) by executing the failed operation a second time. This is usually performed by the I/O subsystem, invisible to the requesting task. Retries are usually successful in dealing with soft errors.

Round Robin Scheduling - A means of scheduling whereby tasks in the Ready List are executed in order, and entries into the Ready List are always put at the end of the list. Usually, each task is also given a limited time for execution. If after this time it is not complete, it is reentered at the end of the Ready List and the next task is executed.

Running - A task state in which the task is executing on a processor.

Save - A system utility that writes a file from secondary storage to a backup volume such as magnetic or paper tape for protection or archival purposes.

Scheduler - A system service that determines which task within the system should be run next.

Scheduling Algorithm - The rule(s) by which the scheduler determines which task in the Ready List should be granted processor time next.

Sector - The smallest contiguous storage area on a magnetic secondary storage medium. In microprocessor systems with flexible diskette drives as the secondary storage medium, sector size is typically 128 bytes.

Segment - An arbitrary user defined block (of data or instructions) that functions as an independent unit. A segment may be placed anywhere in memory and its contents accessed by segment name and relative location within the segment. Some computer systems implement segmentation in hardware via a Base Register (to contain the starting address of the segment), with all segment accesses occurring relative to the segment starting address.

Segment Table - A table that describes all segments of a task and is used by the operating system for memory allocation, relocation, and paging.

Self-Modifying Code - A section of computer instructions whose execution has as one of its effects, the modification of one or more of the instructions within that section. Note that self-modifying code cannot be stored in ROM/PROM.

Semaphore - A "gating" variable that is used to synchronize task operations on shared data. A semaphore permits only a single task to access shared data at any given time - all other tasks are locked out until the first task unlocks the shared data. By operating on semaphores with two well defined functions (called P and V), a task may request and release exclusive access to shared data.

Send - A system service used for task communication and synchronization that places a message in the appropriate mailbox. If a task is waiting at the mailbox, it is placed in the Ready List.

Glossary 131

Sequential Access File - A type of file structure in which data may only be accessed sequentially, one record at a time. Data stored on magnetic tape is an example of a sequential file.

Serially Reusable Resource - A resource, such as a printer or terminal, which may be used by another task as soon as the current task is finished using it. Typically a task requests the resource, the operating system allocates the resource to the task, the task uses the resource, and finally the task releases the resource back to the operating system.

Shared Data - Data in memory or on a secondary storage device that is used by more than one task.

Soft Error - A dynamic error normally caused by some transient condition. Retrying the failed operation will often result in successful completion.

Source File - A text input file for a language translator.

Spooler - A system program that permits I/O transfers to be queued for an I/O device, thereby permitting the requesting task to continue executing even when it cannot immediately use the I/O device. Spoolers are commonly used with very slow sequential *output only* devices such as printers.

Squeeze - Another term for Garbage Collection.

Start - A system service that enters a task into the Ready List so that it is ready to be executed. Some operating systems permit tasks to be started at a specified time-of-day, after a preset interval, or periodically.

Stop - A system service which deletes a task from the Ready List so that it will no longer be executed.

Static Priority - A form of scheduling in which a task's execution priority is fixed either when the task is loaded or at SYSGEN time. This priority remains unchanged as the task executes.

Suspended - A task state in which task execution is discontinued pending the occurrence of an event.

Swapping - A feature of an operating system which permits suspended tasks to be moved to secondary storage in order to generate enough memory space so that the next task on the Ready List can be loaded into memory (if it is not already resident) and executed. The task will be swapped back into system memory when it is scheduled to resume execution. This movement to and from secondary storage may occur many times to a given task before its executing is complete.

Symbolic Debugger - A system software interactive debugging utility in which the debugging software has access to program symbol tables and a programmer can refer to memory location names rather than absolute addresses. This is an extremely valuable facility for use with relocatable code or paged systems where task code may not be loaded at the same memory address each time it executes.

Synchronization - The process of coordinating the execution of tasks within an operating system. Access to shared data as well as the transmission and reception of messages requires this coordination.

SYSGEN - An abbreviation for System Generation.

System Generation - The process of generating, linking and loading all required system modules together in order to build a new operating system or to update tables in an existing system. Because of installation environment variations, it is often necessary to make modifications to an operating system (as shipped by the supplier) in order to configure it for a particular installation. These modifications may include I/O device specifications and memory/disk size definitions. Modern operating systems supply a SYSGEN utility that asks questions about the installation through the system console. The answers, as input by the operator, are checked against known design limits and the utility essentially builds a new operating system from the data it receives.

System Service - Functions such as timekeeping, memory allocation, and console I/O that the operating system performs for user tasks upon request.

System Software - Software that is intimately associated with the operating system, e.g., kernel routines, system services and system support software.

System Support - Functions such as language translators, debugging tools, diagnostics, and libraries which enable a system user or programmer to write and test tasks in an efficient manner.

Target Machine - The final machine on which a program is to run. The target machine may not be the same computer on which the program was implemented and debugged. This is often the case with microprocessor systems.

Task - A software module in which code is executed in a sequential manner.

Task Control Block - Another term for a Task Descriptor.

Task Descriptor - A block of task information that is manipulated by the system and often stored in system tables to increase scheduling efficiency. This information includes the task name, number, priority, and state, as well as other pertinent status data.

Task List - A system data structure containing a list of tasks within the system.

Task State - The status of a task; it may be undefined, ready to execute, executing, or suspended awaiting some event.

Throughput - The quantity of information processed by a computer system in a unit time. This quantity is frequently used for system comparisons. For example, a communication system with a throughput of 50 messages per second is superior to a system with a throughput of 25 messages per second.

Thrashing - The point of system collapse in which operating system overhead is so large that no useful task execution can be accomplished. This occurs often in virtual storage systems when so many users are on the system that every time the system attempts to service a user, a page fault occurs, and the system is constantly attempting to load/reload pages from secondary storage.

Time - A system service that supplies the current time to requesting tasks.

Timer - A hardware device that supplies interrupts on an interval or time-of-day basis to the operating system.

Time Sharing - A type of operating system that supports more than one user concurrently, and allows each user to interact with his job. This is done by allocating processor and resources to each user in turn for a small period of time, thus assuring each user a system response within a few seconds. This philosophy is almost the exact opposite of a Batch system.

Time Slice - That period of time, normally 1-50 milliseconds, allocated to each task in a time sharing system.

Glossary

Trace - A system utility used in software debugging that records instruction execution. This may occur in real time, as with some microcomputer development systems or instruction execution may be simulated at a much slower rate. A programmer can then retrace program execution at his desk and correct errors.

Track - The storage area on a rotating secondary storage medium such as a disk drive defined by one complete revolution of the medium and no head movement. In microprocessor systems using an IBM standard soft-sectored single density diskette, a track is 26 sectors, or 3328 data bytes.

TSS - An abbreviation for Time Sharing System.

Tuning - Trial, observation, and improvement of system performance by modifying operating system parameters (buffer sizes, memory pools, etc.) and rewriting software modules where required.

Turn-Around Time - The interval between the time a program/job is submitted and the time it is completed.

Undefined - A task state in which the task is unknown to the operating system. This means that the task descriptor information has not been entered into the system tables. A task is in this state before it has been created and after it has been deleted from the system.

Utility - A task generally supplied with the operating system which performs widely used standard functions such as file save and restore, disk compression, file copy, etc.

V - A primitive and indivisible operation that is used by a task when it exits a critical section. This operation opens the semaphore "gate" and allows one and only one waiting task to enter the critical section. If no tasks are waiting, the gate remains open for the next task that wishes access.

Virtual Memory - A technique that separates the logical address space from the physical address space. This permits an application program to be written and executed independent of the available physical memory.

Virtual Storage - Another term for Virtual Memory.

Volume - A unit of secondary storage media such as a magnetic tape, disk pack, or flexible diskette.

Wait - A system service that causes a task to be suspended for a specified time or pending the occurrence of an event. It is also used to refer to the task state in which execution is suspended pending the occurrence of an event. When used in conjunction with mailboxes for task communication and synchronization, the wait service causes a task to wait (enter the suspended state) at a mailbox for the next message. If a message is currently in the mailbox, the task receives the message and continues executing.

Wait List - A list of tasks waiting for an event or message at a mailbox. Each mailbox has a separate wait list. If a message is present in the mailbox when a task utilizes the *wait* system service, the message is passed to the task. On the other hand, if no message is in the mailbox or if there are tasks currently in the wait list for the mailbox, the requesting task is suspended and placed at the end of the wait list.

Wakeup - The act of making a task ready to run after a period of suspension.

Working Set - That set of pages in a virtual memory system which a given task references in a specified period of time. In order to run the task without page faults, its working set must be in memory when it is restarted.

Appendix B

References

Brinch Hansen, P., The Architecture of Concurrent Programs, Prentice-Hall, Inc., New Jersey, 1977.

Brinch Hansen, P., Operating System Principles, Prentice-Hall, Inc., New Jersey, 1973.

Flores, I., Computer Software: Programming Systems for Digital Computers, Prentice-Hall, Inc., New Jersey, 1965.

Kleinrock, L., Queueing Systems, Vol. 1: Theory, Wiley Interscience, 1975.

Kleinrock, L., Queueing Systems, Vol. 2: Computer Applications, Wiley Interscience, 1976.

Knuth, D. E., Fundamental Algorithms, Addison-Wesley Publishing Company, Massachusetts, 1975.

Shaw, A. C., The Logical Design of Operating Systems, Prentice-Hall, Inc., New Jersey, 1974.

Stimler, S., Real-Time Data-Processing Systems, McGraw-Hill, Inc., New York, 1969.

Watson, R. W., Time Sharing System Design Concepts, McGraw-Hill, Inc., New York, 1970.

Wilkes, M. V., Time Sharing Computer Systems, American Elsevier Inc., New York, 1975.

INDEX

Abstract Machine, 39
Accept, 57
Accounting, 50
Allocate, 67
Assembler, 21-24, 39
Assign, 34, 67
Associative Memory, 74
Attach, 74
Attributes, 91-93

Backspace, 91
Base Register, 71
Batch, 8-9
Best Fit, 69
Bit Map, 91
Blocked (See Suspended)
Breakpoint, 45
Buffer Memory, 79
Busy Wait, 56

Capability, 91-93, 98-101
Capability Segment, 100
Chaining, 81
Checksum, 81
Class, 98
Close, 34
Communication, 30, 33, 53
Compiler, 41-42
Compress, 47 (See also Garbage Collection)
Consumable Resource, 66
Consumer, 66
Content-Addressable Memory (See Associative Memory)

Context, 24-26
Copy, 47
Create, 31-32
Critical Region (See Critical Section)
Critical Section, 55
Cycle Stealing, 79

Data Structure, 30
Date, 31
Deadlock, 74-75
Debugger, 43-46
Delete, 32
Demand Paging, 73
Device Driver, 34, 78
Diagnostics, 49
Direct I/O, 78-80
Directory, 46, 88
Dispatcher (See Scheduler)
Distributed Processing, 16-17
DMA, 79
Dual Port Memory, 79
Dynamic Priority, 61

Editor, 43
Entry Point, 24
Error Code, 81
Event Flag, 55
Executive (See Operating System)
Exchange (See Mailbox)

FIFO, 61
File, 88, 89, 93
File System, 84-94
First Fit, 69
First-In First-Out (See FIFO)
Foreground/Background, 11

Fragmentation, 69
Free, 67
Friendly Environment, 35

Garbage Collection, 68, 89
General Services, 30-31

Hard Error, 81
High Level Language, 39
Hostile Environment, 35

In Circuit Emulation (ICE), 46
Index Table, 91
Indirect I/O, 78-80
Install, 49
Interactive Debugger, 45-46
Interleaving, 87
Interleave Factor, 87
Interpreter, 39-41
Interval Timer, 62
I/O Channel (See I/O Processor)
I/O Executive (See I/O Subsystem)
I/O Facilities, 46-47
I/O Mapped, 78
I/O Processor, 14-15
I/O Subsystem, 80-82
I/O Supervisor (See I/O Subsystem)

JCL (See Job Control Language)
Job Control Language, 4

Kernel, 5

Language Translator, 38-39
Length Register, 71, 98
Library, 47
Linked List, 30, 54
Linker, 43
Loader, 43
Load Module, 43
Load Sharing, 16
Logical Address, 73
Logical Device, 80
Log On, 96

Mailbox, 54, 55, 56-57
Memory Dump, 44
Memory Management, 70
Memory Mapped, 78
Message, 53-54
Microcomputer Development System, 38
Monitor, 5, 98
Multiprocessing, 14-15
Multiprogramming, 4, 12-13
Multitasking (See Multiprogramming)
Multiterminal, 13
Multiuser, 13

Non-Preemptive Scheduling, 60-61
Nucleus, 5

Object Code, 43
Open, 34

Operating System, 3-4
  batch, 8-9
  real time, 9-12
  multiprogramming, 12-13
  multiuser, 13
  multiprocessing, 14-15
Overhead, 63-64
Overlay, 73

P, 55-56
Page, 70, 72-73
Page Fault, 73
Performance Monitoring, 50
Physical Address, 73
Physical Device, 80
Pool, 68
Preemptive Scheduling, 60, 61-63
Priority Scheduling, 61 (See also Preemptive Scheduling)
Privileged, 35, 97
Process (See Task)
Producer, 66
Protection Violation, 72, 98

Queue, 30, 56

Random Access, 91
Ready, 26-27
Ready List, 32-33
Real Time, 9-12
Real Time Clock, 61
Record, 88
Reentrant Code, 25
Release, 34, 67

Resource, 66 (See also Resource Services)
Resource Services, 30, 34
Response Time, 62
Restore, 47
Retry, 81
Round Robin Scheduling, 61-62
Running, 26, 28

Save, 47
Scheduler, 24, 27, 33, 60
Sector, 85
Security, 30, 35
Segment, 70
Self-Modifying Code, 25
Semaphore, 55-56
Send, 57
Sequential Access, 91
Serially Reusable Resource, 66
Soft Error, 81
Spooler, 82
Squeeze (See Garbage Collection)
Start, 32
Stop, 32
Static Priority, 61
Suspended, 26, 28
Swapping, 25
Symbolic Debugger, 46
Synchronization, 54
SYSGEN (See System Generation)
System Generation, 48-49
System Service, 30-35

Index   143

System Service, 30-35
    general services, 30-31
    task services, 30, 31-33
    communication, 30, 33
    resource services, 30, 34
    security, 30, 35
System Software, 2
System Support, 30, 38-50
    language translators, 38-39
    parogram editing & loading, 42-43
    debugging, 43-56
    I/O facilities, 46-47
    libraries, 47
    system generation, 48-49
    diagnostics, 49
    performance monitoring, 50
System Security, 96-101

Task, 20-28
Task Control Block (See Task Descriptor.
Task Descriptor, 24
Task List, 31-32
Task Services, 30, 31-33
Task State, 26-28
    undefined, 26, 27
    ready, 26-27
    running, 26, 28
    suspended, 26, 28
Thrashing, 74, 75-76
Time, 31
Time Sharing, 13, 62
Time Slice, 62
Trace, 45
Track, 85
TSS (See Time Sharing System)
Turn-Around Time, 9

Undefined, 26-27
Utility, 38

V, 55-56
Virtual Memory, 73-74
Virtual Storage (See Virtual Memory)
Volume, 88

Wait, 31, 57
Working Set, 76